AT FULL BRIGHTNESS

AT FULL BRIGHTNESS

A NOVEL

THANH-THẢO SUE ĐỖ

NEW DEGREE PRESS

COPYRIGHT © 2021 THANH-THẢO SUE ĐỖ

All rights reserved.

AT FULL BRIGHTNESS

A Novel

ISBN	978-1-63730-443-3	*Paperback*
	978-1-63730-543-0	*Kindle Ebook*
	978-1-63730-544-7	*Ebook*

*To all the parents who have complex relationships with their children,
may we know them, may we love them, may
we embrace them with all their flaws.
May we as sons and daughters find our way
to heal and bond as time goes by.
May we explore ourselves while our parents hold on to the once
little children they had held only in memories and pictures.
But most of all,
to my mom and dad,
this is for you.*

CONTENTS

	AUTHOR'S NOTE	11
CHAPTER 1.	ROOTS	15
CHAPTER 2.	TINY BUT MIGHTY	21
CHAPTER 3.	I'VE GOT MILES TO GO	33
CHAPTER 4.	TEMPORARY PAIN BUT GREATER GAIN	39
CHAPTER 5.	NOT YOUR TYPICAL MATH STUDENT	53
CHAPTER 6.	EMERGENCE	63
CHAPTER 7.	FINDING MYSELF	73
CHAPTER 8.	DELIBERATION	83
CHAPTER 9.	POWERLESS	93
CHAPTER 10.	IT TAKES A VILLAGE	101
CHAPTER 11.	AN OPPORTUNITY	111
CHAPTER 12.	BOUNDARIES AND SPIRITUAL COMFORT	119
CHAPTER 13.	A MOTHER'S PAIN	127
CHAPTER 14.	PANIC ATTACK	133
CHAPTER 15.	SURVIVAL MODE	143
CHAPTER 16.	IT TAKES COURAGE TO FACE THE TRUTH	151
CHAPTER 17.	SPIRITUAL MENTORING	159
CHAPTER 18.	THE EPIPHANY	165
CHAPTER 19.	BUMPS AND PROGRESS	171
CHAPTER 20.	HEALING THE WOUNDS	183
CHAPTER 21.	A HOPEFUL FUTURE	191
CHAPTER 22.	AT FULL BRIGHTNESS	199
	ACKNOWLEDGMENTS	205

Do not lose courage in considering your own imperfections.
—ST. FRANCIS DE SALES

AUTHOR'S NOTE

Dear Reader,

The words in this fictional novel are the result of my own journey. When I was nine years old, I started journaling my poems despite still learning English while immigrating over to the United States five years earlier. When I was in junior high, my teacher had my classmates and I write about our lives in the form of a memoir. From that memoir, I knew I had found my calling as a writer. Somehow, the words I wrote gave me comfort from the hardships of adjusting to life's twists and turns.

I was born with cerebral palsy and am a disabled Vietnamese daughter of immigrant parents. I struggled with depression and anxiety, and I lost my faith at one point, but I have grown stronger through the support of many people.

As a daughter of Vietnamese parents who stressed the importance of success being molded into a career, I wanted to show that having your own pursuits and passions can lead to a better well-being. I am sure many of us in our communities can relate to these issues. My hope is this book will inspire conversations around following our own callings, gaining confidence in pursuing therapy, leaning on prayer and spirituality to get through difficult times, and building a strong network of support through family, friends, and mentors.

Mental health topics are perceived as "taboo" in many cultures and groups, which may lead to many young people hesitating to get the support they need. This can keep them from moving forward with life or pursuing their heart's calling. Wouldn't we want to pursue something we love and practice mental wellness? I believe so, and if you do as well, this story is for you.

The characters in this book are based on my own experiences and deal with issues like disability, building relationships, mental health, and faith.

In overcoming the many obstacles I faced, I discovered what success truly means for me. When you do what you love, it will spark joy and passion for you. Other people in your life will see that joy, and it will show in your emotions, mannerisms, and the way you interact with people around you.

That joy is what makes us want to do more for others. A lot of us are trapped in the idea that success is a career with a lot of monetary rewards and honor, especially among immigrant parents who expect a lot. This perception can lead to regretting career choices, self-esteem issues, and mental health struggles. Then there are those like myself who also suffer from a disability, which can bring about a whole set of different expectations and challenges to navigate.

These issues can affect the way we see ourselves.

I hope to normalize conversations about mental health within the Asian-American and Pacific Islander community and foster a better understanding of these issues.

Whatever our calling may be, all of us are here to tap into our gifts to contribute to the world. For some of us who believe in a higher power, or God, there is that gift waiting for you. My mental health struggles and personal desires were always left on the back burner. As a result, I turned to spirituality and prayer and sought out professional help for my mental health issues.

This book seeks to explore the intersections between disability, mental health, relationships, and faith, reconciling three ideas:
1. Happiness comes from following your heart.
2. It is okay to talk about mental health issues.
3. Your faith and getting treatment for mental health issues is a sign of strength and vulnerability.

Each of us are capable of loving and being loved.

This is a story about rekindling oneself, belonging, acceptance, and forgiveness. It is a story of hope and faith—something we all can rely on in tough times—and the relationships we build with our families, friends, and mentors.

I hope you all enjoy this book as much as I enjoyed writing it. It is written for you, for me, and for those who need a space to belong. With all that said, I'll leave you with this to reflect on:

Follow your heart because it will never lead you wrong.

Happy reading!

All my best,

Thanh-Thảo Sue Do

CHAPTER 1

ROOTS

My mother and father once told me the story of how I came about as the youngest child in a family of six siblings. It was years later when I thought to ask about the parts of my childhood I could not remember.

I was born a preemie, the size of a sixteen-ounce Nestle water bottle, at Hope Hospital. Surrounded by white walls and numerous tubes from head to foot, my blue face was a dominating feature as I had yet to take my first breath; I was silent and unable to move. The sound of hurried footsteps filled the air as my doctor and the nurses scrambled to find a way to get me to cry.

"Come on, baby girl, come on. Cry for your mama!" The doctor reached into the neonatal intensive care crib I had been placed in, gently touching me. I let out a weak cry, kicking my tiny legs to signal I was alive. My mother turned to look at me with tears in her eyes, her shoulders falling back as she let out a sigh of relief; she knew all the agony she had just experienced was worth it to see her baby girl was okay.

My parents named me *Mai* after the Vietnamese New Year's golden apricot blossom, a symbol of hope and prosperity. The time of my birth was announced at 1:43 p.m. on Valentine's Day, a whole two months earlier than my original expected due date in April. As soon as the doctor brought me to my parents, they gasped at how tiny I was. I could fit into my mother's hand despite the multiple blankets that had been used to wrap me. My mother held me for a bit before a nurse dressed in blue, flowery scrubs came to take me to the NICU room to be put on a ventilator and under light to treat my jaundice.

"When will we get to go home?" my mother asked the doctor while grasping my father's hand. She frowned slightly, her lips shaking.

"If things go well with your daughter, she may be able to go home in a month and a half. But if they don't go well, maybe even longer. Rest assured, we are doing the best we can to treat her and keep her safe and healthy." He glanced at the heartbeat monitor.

"All right, doc. I trust you," my mother said. She looked down, marveling at me. On the outside, my mother appeared calm, even serene perhaps, but on the inside she was plagued with worry and doubt. *Will Mai be able to breathe on her own? Will she be able to feed on her own instead of getting milk from a tube?*

"Ah!" my father beamed proudly to my mother.

Each day was a struggle for me to breathe in the NICU because of my underdeveloped lungs. I fought to make my entrance into the world earlier than most babies. I didn't grow much either and all my clothes were bigger than my body, so my mother altered the onesies to fit me.

A month later, when the doctors decided I could go home, my parents walked out hand in hand with me buckled in a gray car seat. On the drive home, I sank into slumber without a care in the world, all bundled up in a pink, wool blanket. A while later, my mother turned the keys to the door of our house and opened it to my oldest sister Như looking up from her schoolwork. My mother held me, walking quietly to my room so as not to wake me up. My nursery room was clean and organized, filled with pink, and had been put together by my five older siblings. I was the newest addition to this close-knit Vietnamese family.

"Wow, I have another baby sister! Full head of hair, beautiful eyes, and great genes! Can I please hold her, Mom?" Như asked with excitement in her eyes.

"Be very careful; your sister's very fragile," my mother said, handing me to Như.

"I will, Mom. I can watch her while you and Dad work from now on."

"Thanks, sweetie. I'll let you know when that can happen. Until then, give yourself a little break from reading. You're stuck in a book every day," my mother said, mindful of my ten-year-old studious sister who was set on her goal of becoming an aspiring physician.

"I'll try," Như said, smiling slightly and fixing the flaps of the blanket on me. As Như and my mother stood together talking, my brother Minh came in from the backyard of our house, heading up the stairs bouncing a basketball up and down with his headphones in his ears. He was about to head to his bedroom and then got distracted by the noise in the nursery. He walked over to Như and Mom and peered down at me, taking off his headphones.

"She looks like a pea, Mom," he remarked snidely. Minh had a loose mentality. He was very easygoing and sometimes a little too boisterous for a nine-year-old. He also had no issue with speaking his mind.

"Shh! Watch your words, son. Mai's your youngest sister, and she's sleeping, so be considerate and take the ball back outside," my mother replied sternly. Minh turned pink in the face and walked back outside, muttering under his breath the whole way, embarrassed. His nine-year-old mind hadn't worked out his new role as my big brother.

Như made a parting gesture to our mother, left the nursery, and then walked over to Linh's room and knocked gently on her door while holding me in her arms.

"Sis? Hey, Linh, we have a surprise. Open up and see," Như said, glancing at me as I continued to sleep without a care in the world. The door opened slightly with a creak and Linh's head poked out.

"What's the surprise?" Linh answered her own question when her gaze fell on me in Như's arms and she smiled widely, eyes glowing in excitement as she took in the sight of me. "Aw, our new baby sis. I'm so in love with her already. Where's Mom?"

"Mom's resting. Let her be. Here, why don't you hold her while I go get Liên and Hồng-an?" Như gently handed me to Linh.

"Sure, Như." Linh took me gently in her arms. "Hey, little sis. It's your big sister Linh." I heard her voice and it stirred me from sleep, my head turning toward the sound slightly though my eyes remained closed. "Aw, you can hear me well, little angel." I opened one eye and stared at her. A moment later, Liên and Hồng-an came in with Như and peered over me.

"What a cutie patootie," Liên said, smiling now. She held out a drawing of me and showed Như.

"That's beautiful," Như said to Liên. "I'm sure Mai likes it." By this point, I had opened my eyes fully and was peering up at my sisters as they gathered closely around me. "Oh look, she opened her eyes!" Hồng-an said, her usual quiet mannerisms falling away in her excitement.

"This is the most I've heard you talk in a while, Hồng-an. Taking a break from your paints?" Như teased, trying to get Hồng-an out of her shell.

"I love babies, Như. I think we all do. Besides, I am not a recluse. Just trying to be an older sister. Mom and Dad already have so much on their hands. I think Mai's the icing on the cake of our lives."

"That's a good metaphor to describe her. I'm impressed, Hồng-an." Như looked on at me.

"Mai is just *so* cute!" Hồng-an exclaimed excitedly. Normally she was the quiet sister in the house; she was eager to meet me. My sisters stood together and continued to gush over me while I stared at them, unaware of all the attention I was getting.

"Mai's definitely getting tired," Như said, walking back to the nursery to hand me back to our mother. She was mature for a ten-year-old, always paying attention to other people's needs.

***

As the months went by and my family settled into the new routine of having a baby in the house, my siblings did their best to help take care of me whenever my parents had to work long hours and needed the extra help. At first, I seemed like any other normal healthy baby, but by the time I was about a year and half old, my parents had noticed that I couldn't even pull myself up into a sitting position, something most babies could do by my age. They also noticed that my legs were drooping and my toes were curled inward. It was enough to cause them some minor worry.

    No matter how I tried to pull myself upward, I would always fall and cry. Whenever my mother heard me crying, she would come to pick me up and, using the corners of her shirt, she would wipe away my tears and comfort me. Then she would often caress my ebony-black hair like a horse's mane and sing Vietnamese songs to me. After a while, whenever I had settled, my mom would put me down again and I would go happily crawling all over the playroom. When I ran out of energy, I would sit up, staring intently at my calloused kneecaps. My big eyes twinkled as my lips curved into a small grin; my young mind was shielded from the hardships that were to come.

CHAPTER 2

TINY BUT MIGHTY

―

The blazing sun showed its rays on the day my parents took me to the doctor. As they closed the door to our house behind them, with me in their arms and a diaper bag in hand, they could not help but wonder what the doctor was going to say about me still crawling and not taking my first steps on time. My father put on a brave face, hiding his anxiety. He buckled me in my car seat while my tiny body resisted, trying to push his arms away.

"Now, now, it's going to be all right. I'm right here," my father said as I wailed louder.

On the drive there, my mother tried to sing my favorite songs to me. She oohed and aahed with me to distract me from crying. She patted and rubbed my toes to relax me.

"Are we almost there yet, honey? Poor Mai. She's so tired." My mother tried to distract me with a funny expression.

"Oh, she'll be fine," my father said, keeping his eyes on the road.

"Oh, good." My mother watched me intently as I babbled on.

Ten minutes later, my parents arrived at a big, white building labeled Pediatrics Department.

My father parked the car in front of the building while my mother held me in her arms with the diaper bag. They walked inside, checked in, and sat down to wait. Soon enough, a cheerful medical assistant wearing smiley-faced sunflower scrubs came out to greet my parents and I.

"Mai Tran?" My father waved his arms to signal we were present. "Nice to meet you. I'm Allison, I'm Dr. Georgeson's medical assistant." She looked at me with warm eyes. "And you must be Mai! Oh my gosh, I like your shirt." She cooed at me. I laughed. "Come right this way."

Allison led us through the halls of the hospital to a door marked *Dr. Dave Georgeson, M.D. Orthopedist Specialist*. She took my weight, measured my height, and checked my temperature. After she noted the information down on my chart, she turned to my parents and smiled. "I will tell the doctor you are here."

My parents held me in their arms, passing me between each other while we waited for the doctor to arrive. Although I was unaware there was even a problem, my parents were very worried about my future. They knew something was wrong with my legs, and they wondered if it would affect my life growing up and whether or not I would be able to function like a normal kid.

Five minutes later, the door opened again and a man in his late forties stepped in. He was dressed in a white coat with round glasses, bald head, blue eyes, and an impressive physical build. Dr. Dave Georgeson came toward my parents, shaking their hands as he greeted them before turning to greet me.

"So, you are Mai, ah! Can you walk for me?" My father took me from my mother's arm and proceeded to help me stand in an upright position. My legs were twitching as he held both of my arms raised. "Let's see if you can walk by yourself, Mai."

My father let go of both of my arms. I felt my body drooping, and then I flopped to the floor. "Oops, up you go." Dr. Georgeson picked me up and checked my legs. He gently bent my legs to see what was going on and then proceeded to check my knees. He held up my legs and stretched them to see how far they could go. I started crying louder as he stretched. The pain gnawed through my muscles and ached. I wailed louder. "Oh, I know. I know. We're almost done. It's all right."

Dr. Georgeson walked over to his drawer and pulled out a small-sized toy ring. "Here you go. This is for you, Mai." He gave me the unicorn toy ring and I stopped crying. I played with the ring while he checked me one more time before handing me back to my parents. He turned to his computer and typed in some notes for additional tests, took a deep breath, and told my parents:

"Your daughter has cerebral palsy. It's *Spastic diplegia cerebral palsy* to be specific. It affects her limbs and the stiffness of her muscles. The good news is that in her case, the cerebral palsy is mild. She will need physical and occupational therapy for the rest of her life, but she will be able to stand up and walk. She will need a walker, and when she gets older, she will need surgery to stretch out her hamstrings to prevent toe-walking. I believe she has a strong will to overcome this. I can already hear it in her wails."

"Doc, will she be able to go to school and participate in the mainstream program?" My father asked, eager to hear Dr. Georgeson's verdict. I stared at my doctor with my big, brown eyes, soaking in what they said even though I could not yet comprehend what was going on.

"Yes, she will be able to. Thankfully, her mentality and her ability to process information will not be affected by cerebral palsy."

"Thank you, Dr. Georgeson." My father stood up, shaking the doctor's hand. My mother did the same.

"It's my pleasure."

We scheduled our next appointment and walked back to the car.

"In you go, my dear." This time I stayed quiet. I did not cry as much as I had that morning. My happiness was the toy ring that Dr. Georgeson gave me. I played with the ring all the way home.

***

The next morning dawned bright and early for my parents, as neither of them had been able to get much sleep fretting over my diagnosis.

"Morning Hung, morning Mai," my mother said, coming down the stairs into the living room. I had already been down with my father playing.

"Morning, Khánh. How did you sleep?" My father replied, looking up at her from the couch. My mother came over and sat next to him. The rest of my siblings were still asleep in their beds.

"Just so-so. How about you?" my mother replied, reaching out to grasp my father's hand for reassurance.

"I've been thinking about Mai's diagnosis all night." My father sighed, shaking his head.

"Yeah, me too. She's going to be okay as long as we get her into therapy as soon as we can," my mother replied, determined.

"You know, you're the best. I am so glad I married you."

"I know, and you were lucky too. My intuition was right all along."

My father chuckled lightly. "Sorry, boss. I should have listened to you."

My mother was hopeful that both occupational and physical therapy would help me regain my mobility. She scheduled an appointment with Andrea, the administrative assistant for the California Children's Place Inc., that very same day. All her sadness and disappointment of me not being immobile lifted; she had high hopes for me to one day walk and become an accomplished daughter somehow. But first, she had to figure out how to immerse me in physical therapy at such a young age.

A week later, my parents drove me to my first therapy session. As they walked in with me in their arms, Andrea greeted us with my new therapist, Jane. Jane was originally from New York but had moved to California to pursue her master's degree in physical and occupational therapy. I was one of her youngest patients at only eighteen months old.

"This is Mai. She's your new patient." Andrea introduced us and then made herself scarce once Jane started introducing herself to me.

"Nice to meet you, Mai. Let me see you walk!" Jane said, extending her arms out. I babbled at my name. There was this joy inside me every time someone called me Mai. My sense of awareness was pretty strong for a toddler.

My mother put me down and Jane observed me intently while taking notes. I heard the stroking of her pen on paper as she wrote quickly. She watched my legs twitching and drooping and my eyes raise up in a daze because I was concentrating too hard.

Thump. Down I fell.

"Whoops, are you okay? C'mon, let's get back up." Jane held on to one of my hands while she had the other hand on my right hip. She put her notes aside on the blue mat and then leaned over to fully support me with both hands. She had me walk with support around the little treatment play area. There were balls rolling around the therapeutic slides and Jane encouraged me to pick up a red ball by bending down and leaning over without falling. "Okay, Mai, I want you to get the ball with one hand without falling over."

Jane didn't expect me to understand but followed my cues and pointed to objects and places so I knew what to do.

She continued to do those exercises with me until the end of my session.

One hour ticked by and at the end of my therapy session, I felt my eyes drooping because I had used up all my energy working my muscles. Jane handed me back to my parents with a list of home exercises I could do.

As soon as we got home from the therapy session, my parents decided to call a family meeting. My father held me in his arms and asked my sister:

"Như, can you call the rest of your siblings to come downstairs? We have an important announcement we want to make."

"What kind of announcement?" Như asked, her eyes perking up.

"You'll find out in a few minutes," my father said, handing me to my mother.

"Okay. Guys! Come downstairs! Mom and Dad have something to tell us!" Như exclaimed. All my siblings ran downstairs, one after the other, and sat around in the living room.

"Let's sit down," my father said, mentally preparing himself. He took a deep breath in and slowly let it out. "Okay, kids. Your little sister... Ahem…" My father paused and took another breath. He looked at my mother, who placed a hand on his shoulder as she held me on her hip. I managed a cute smile as my eyes lit up at the sight of my siblings.

"Dad? Is Mai okay?" Hồng-an asked, looking anxious as the minutes went by. She glanced at the clock in the kitchen corner.

"Recently, we took your sister to a doctor to find out why she has trouble walking and we got an official diagnosis," my father said, keeping a straight face.

"What is it?" Như asked, eager to know.

"It's called cerebral palsy. It's a condition that makes the muscles tight. Mai will be able to walk, but she will fall often because her muscles won't work the same way as all of yours," my father responded calmly.

"Oh," Minh had a bored look on his face. "Does that mean I have to help her?"

"What kind of question is that, Minh? Of course we do. We're her older siblings," Như chastised.

"Is the meeting over?" he asked, fidgeting in his seat, attempting to make his escape.

"No, Minh, you are not leaving this table until I give you permission," my mother said, glancing at him sternly.

"Aww," Minh responded with a disappointed look on his face.

"Yeah, Minh, stay where you are." Linh gave him a warning look. Hồng-an and Liên sat still and didn't utter a word.

"Mai will need a lot of help and support, and I expect you all to be kind and caring to her. She is your younger sister," my father said, adjusting his glasses.

"Okay," all of my siblings said in unison. I babbled in my mother's arms.

"Meeting adjourned." My father got up from the table and went to the bedroom. My mother walked upstairs to put me to bed while my siblings went back to their rooms.

From that meeting onward, Như would set aside some time every day after studying to help me complete my home exercises when my parents worked.

"Here's a ball for you, baby." Như held the ball and squeezed it for me. I reached over and grabbed the ball, observing her and copied what she did. I gave her one of my biggest grins and nodded. As Như pulled me up, I could feel my arm slipping back down. She sat with me in my nursery, watching me and making sure I was focused on my exercises. Occasionally, she would reach and hold other objects for me, and then we would do our stretches together. As I was standing, I felt my knees shaking once again and I landed flat on the floor.

I had fallen again.

"Oops, you okay, baby?" Như asked, extending both arms out to prevent me from slipping again. "Minh, come help Mai exercise! Mom's busy, and Mai needs to keep up with her benchmark goals so she'll improve her mobility."

Minh groaned from his room. "Do I have to? I am playing Minecraft! Such a nuisance!"

"Minh, I am not telling you again. Mom's busy," Như said, raising her eyebrows.

"Fine, I'll do it, but have Mom pay me ten dollars when she gets home from work," Minh bargained. He came and sat down on the floor with me, picking up the ball and rolling it toward me with some force, where it hit my foot hard. I fell again, but this time I landed flat on my face and started crying.

"Minh, you need to be gentle with Mai!" Như picked me up and rubbed my face. She gave Minh a warning look. "This is all on you." Như bent down at Minh's eye level.

"C'mon, it's not that bad," Minh pleaded, hoping to get out of the situation.

"Sometimes I don't know where you get your energy from. Did any of the words from the meeting ever get to you? Mai's legs don't work the same way yours do!" Như's voice rose, close to anger now.

"Okay, sorry, Mai. High five?" Minh asked, looking at me in Như's arms. I turned away and buried my face in Như's shoulder, wetting her shirt with my tears.

Minh grimaced after I looked away from him. On his way out, he picked up his basketball and bounced it out into the backyard, closing the door behind him, mumbling his apology under his breath.

The front door creaked open and my mother came in, immediately noticing my tear-stained face. She took off her shoes, hung up her purse, and came toward me. My mother looked concerned when she noticed I wasn't my usual self.

"What is going on, Như? Why is Mai crying? Did she fall?" She moved toward Như as she spoke.

"No, it's fine. It was a little rough play. Mai's okay. Right, sis?" I spread my arms out toward my mother and she pulled me from Như's grasp into her arms.

"I got her. Thanks for helping me today, Như."

"I'm going back to my studies. Let me know if you need help, Mom." Như turned and walked upstairs to her room.

***

It would be another month before I found myself back in Dr. Georgeson's office again. Between my physical therapy sessions with Jane and all the help my siblings had been with my home exercises, my ability to walk had improved greatly. Dr. Georgeson was very happy to see my wonderful progress on my return.

"How's Mai? Up you go!" Dr. Georgeson greeted my family cheerfully. "Let's see you walk again." He reached out and held both of my arms. I walked steadily this time without falling as much.

"Let me write a prescription for her leg braces. The great news is she is walking better now that we have the therapy program in place for her. I am reading over Jane's notes and I see Mai is making great progress with her weekly sessions in therapy."

Dr. Georgeson smiled as he spoke to us. I stared at him with astonishment. Although I was still early in my walking journey, this progress meant my treatment was headed in the right direction.

"Oh, thanks, Doc. She has been working so hard on her exercises. All her siblings are a great help," my mother said, smiling broadly.

"Keep up the great work and be sure to contact Jane or me if you have any questions or concerns about Mai's progress. I want to congratulate you all for being so involved and taking such good care of Mai. That helps me a lot when you are involved," Dr. Georgeson said.

"Thank you so much for taking such good care of our daughter," my father said, shaking Dr. Georgeson's hand as he picked me up. Dr. Georgeson smiled and walked to his cabinet where he pulled out another toy ring for me. This time, there was a bear on top of the ring. I grabbed hold of the ring and played with it. That was our routine for every appointment after that.

Time went by as I continued my therapy sessions. Each day was a new success for me as I learned new exercises and made progress. Eventually, Dr. Georgeson prescribed me new braces. The new braces gave me a newfound freedom as I walked as often as I could whenever I could. Jane always reminded me to put one foot in front of the other when I walked, and that's how I would approach each day as well.

I developed a strong gait pattern, putting one foot in front of the other as I practiced walking in my braces outside in my backyard and in public places. I fell often, but every step I took was like conquering a mountain to me; it nurtured my inner determination.

CHAPTER 3

I'VE GOT MILES TO GO

—

SIX YEARS LATER

One day, the summer I turned seven, my mother and I were sitting at the kitchen table together when she got a phone call from our therapy clinic. Jane was involved in a car accident and she would not be coming into work for a while. My mother spoke a while with the receptionist as I sat waiting for her to finish the phone call, listening as she rescheduled my physical therapy appointment for next week with a different therapist named Anne.

"Mom?" I said as I gestured toward her. My mother made eye contact with me, paused, and collected herself before speaking.

"Mai, what's up?" I could see she was struggling to find the right words to tell me what was going on.

"Am I getting a new therapist?" I asked, leaning toward her and looking directly at her eyes.

"Yes, Mai. You're getting a new therapist. This therapist will be just as good as Jane. She will help you walk better too. You'll be fine," my mother said, putting her arms around me. She caressed my hair a bit before letting go.

"Okay," I nodded, satisfied with her answer. I got up again and practiced walking around the living room while my mother looked on from behind me, deep in thought.

I knew walking wasn't easy because every time I took a step, my legs expended more energy, requiring more muscles to work together.

***

The following week, my mother drove me to the therapy clinic. I had gotten used to going to therapy, even though I still resisted and whined every time the appointment day came. Today was going to be a particularly hard day because I was going to meet my new therapist now that Jane would not be returning to work, and I was anxious; I did not like change.

My mother parked the car while I unbuckled myself. She walked around to my side of the car and helped me get out and stand up. Holding on to my arms and glancing at the curb in front of her, she helped guide me toward the door of the clinic. As my mother opened the door, a middle-aged woman dressed in a floral shirt and jeans spoke up with a pleasant tone.

"Hi, Mai! Nice to meet you. I am Anne, your new therapist. I read your files and Jane's notes and I can see you are doing very well." She reached out to shake my mom's hand as she spoke and then reached out to shake mine. Instead of shaking her hand, I pulled out my favorite toy ring and held it up for her to see.

"Look at my toy ring!" I said, bragging to Anne.

"Wow, who gave that to you, Mai?"

"Dr. Georgeson," I beamed with a huge smile on my face. I could talk about the great connection I had with my doctor if I had all day.

"Wow, I can already tell he is your favorite!" Anne winked at me and led me over to a new treatment room. It had a blue mat on the floor with a beam swing attached to the wall. She helped me onto the beam swing and we swung together while she kept her arms behind my back to keep it straight.

"Reach, reach, reach!" Anne encouraged me to stretch both my arms while she swung her legs back and forth to move the swing

"I can't do this!" I wailed, fighting back the urge to put my arms down.

"You're doing it, you're doing it!" Anne cheered me on. Sweat permeated my face and my body started losing momentum. I felt the tears coming faster and faster until they dripped all the way to the floor.

"Oh, Mai, sweetie, you got this! Don't cry. You got this."

"No! It's too hard!" I started attempting to push her away because that's how stubborn I was. I just didn't want to do it anymore. "No, Miss Anne!" I wailed even louder. Anne raised her eyebrows at me, unmoved by my persistence to test her boundaries. I started getting really quiet, assuming she'd give in.

"Hmm… What do you think you're doing, young lady?" Anne helped me off the beam swing and bent down to my eye level. "I am trying to help you, Mai. These exercises will help you walk better." She tried to calm me down, but my stubborn refusal to cooperate persisted. After trying to reason with me and failing, Anne went to get my mother.

A moment later, my mother walked in with Anne from the waiting room. She got down onto my level and stared at me, her gaze intense.

"What's going on, Mai?" my mother asked.

"I don't want to do this anymore. It's so hard and it hurts so much! I wanna go home, Mom!" My mom raised her eyebrows at me in disbelief.

"You can do this, Mai. You are choosing not to cooperate with Miss Anne and making things harder. She's trying to help you," my mom chastised.

"But I don't want to! I'm tired," I pleaded, my eyes staring wider like a begging puppy.

"Just another thirty minutes and you'll be done," my mother tried to reason with me.

"No!" I persisted.

"Don't speak to me like that, Mai!" Her stern voice meant things were about to get serious. My mom grabbed my hand firmly and marched me to the mat where Miss Anne had stayed back to wait.

"Apologize nicely to Miss Anne," my mother insisted. I looked down at the ground instead of at Miss Anne, pouting and wishing I could just disappear instead of apologize. After a few tense, silent moments, I finally relented.

"Sorry, Miss Anne." I shifted nervously in front of her. Anne smiled warmly at me in response to my apology, bending down to my level so she could make eye contact with me.

"Thank you, Mai," she said. "I know these exercises can be hard, but we have to do them so we can help you get stronger and walk better. I know you are a strong girl, so will you try again with me?"

"Yes, Miss Anne." I hugged her now, feeling remorseful for my earlier behavior and ready to try again. The rest of the session went by without any more disruptions or outbursts from me.

***

Anne became my new regular therapist and we continued to have sessions together, each one more difficult than the last. Anne would often push me to my limits but instead of pushing back or getting upset, I would persevere through those long appointments and felt proud of my accomplishments each time. One day, many sessions later, I took my first real steps without any assistance and it dawned on me that I could finally walk.

My parents had taken me to this physical therapy appointment along with all my siblings to see my great progress.

"Tuck your tummy in and remember 'one foot in front of the other.' Go slow and take it one step at a time. You can do it, Mai!" Anne encouraged me, holding me from behind. I could feel the nerves in my feet working as I lifted them slowly but steadily. "There you go, walk to your sister! Walk to Như! Let's go!" Anne cheered me on, her voice rising with excitement as she let me go and I wobbled my way over to my sister all on my own.

When I got to Như, she hugged me tight, exclaiming, "Look at my baby sister go! You're mighty Mai!" Her face lit with joy as my parents recorded this milestone on their phone cameras.

My mother and father both wiped away their happy tears, shouting, "Look at our baby. She did it. She walked!"

"Wow!" Minh finally took notice and looked up from his game on his phone, looking rather impressed with me for the first time I could remember.

"Great job today, Mai. We're so proud of you. Keep working on your exercises, and you'll get even stronger." Anne came over and gave me a high five before locking her arms around me in a tight embrace.

My family and I walked out of the session with relief washing over us. *I had finally walked.*

CHAPTER 4

TEMPORARY PAIN BUT GREATER GAIN

I was ten years old when I learned that life was not all easy and carefree as I had thought. On a bright Wednesday morning, my parents drove me to Hope Hospital once again. As soon as the car rolled into the hospital parking lot, I unbuckled my seat belt clumsily and pushed my door open.

"Slow down, Mai. Careful, don't trip. Do you need a hand?" my mother asked. She reached out to offer me her arm, but I waved it away and walked in front of her.

My father caught up to us and whispered in my mother's ear. "I think she can handle it, Khánh. Sometimes, I think you worry too much about her."

I turned. "What are you both saying?"

"Oh, keep walking, sweetie. We're almost there." my mother said, keeping a cheerful tone. Sure enough, it was only a short walk until we got into the hospital and headed straight for the elevator. We arrived on the third floor at the pre-surgery unit of the Orthopedic Department, where there were rows of green chairs in the waiting room. A medical assistant came out to greet us and lead us back to the exam room. I ran to the examination table and hopped up.

"Wow, I thought you were going to fall, Mai," my mother said. Before I could reply, the door opened and Dr. Georgeson entered the room, greeting us as he sat down and turned on his computer. My mother moved to stand beside me as I sat on the exam table, placing a comforting hand on my shoulder as we waited for what the doctor had to say.

"Mai, we're going to do a surgery on your hamstrings to help lengthen them. Lengthening your hamstrings will help you to walk better, keep you from tripping so often and, the best part, you won't walk on your toes anymore," Dr. Georgeson said, glancing at my chart.

"Really?" I let out a happy yelp like one of those crazy fans worshiping their idol at a concert. He smiled at me and his eyes twinkled.

"Really," he said with a casual grin.

"Will it hurt, Dr. Georgeson?" I asked, hoping for some reassurance.

"It won't hurt because you'll be sedated and we'll wake you up when we are done."

"Okay, I hope I make it out alive!"

My mother looked at me straight in the eye and said, "Mai, we're here for you. We've always been here for you. This is a surgery to help you walk better and I know you are going to be tough as nails."

My father chimed in, "Don't forget that someday you'll be a great pharmacist when all this pain passes."

"What's a pharmacist?" I asked, my eyes growing wider with curiosity.

"It's the role of someone who explains and distributes medications to patients. You know how there are sick people who doctors take care of and write prescriptions for the medication? The patient takes that prescription to a pharmacist who fills the prescription and makes sure the patient gets the medicine their doctor prescribed. This is important because it is for the health of the patients," my mother explained. Dr. Georgeson looked amused as my mother responded to my question.

"Oh, okay." I nodded, unaware that years later, being a pharmacist would not be what I wanted to do.

"So, here's the plan. Next month, we are going to go ahead with the surgery but first, I want to schedule you for a pre-surgery appointment. In this appointment, you and your family are going to hear how to prepare for the surgery, what to bring for the day of the surgery, and how long you'll be staying in the hospital. Any questions?" Dr Georgeson kept a straight face as he waited for my parents to respond.

My father asked him about the procedure and nodded while Dr. Georgeson explained it to him. I sat in silence, listening to the conversation happening between my parents and the doctor but not really understanding what exactly they were talking about. I was just excited to not walk on my toes anymore. I could not help but wonder if I would be a *normal* kid who could walk steadily on her own without assistance. I gritted my teeth nervously, trying to keep my hands together.

My mother turned and looked at me, squinting her eyes in concern.

"What's going on?" she asked me.

"Nothing." I looked away from her. I was worried about how I would walk steadily like other kids. I couldn't see how I could do that.

***

My parents and I walked into the hospital armed with our important documents along with my medical ID and a list of questions they wanted to ask the pre-surgery nurse. We sat down in the waiting room as I felt my heart beating faster. I shook as I watched patients go in and out of the exam room. Each medical assistant who passed by wore the same blue scrubs. I closed my eyes and breathed deeply to calm down. Sure enough, I heard my name being called.

"Mai Tran?" A woman in her mid-thirties walked out, spotted my parents waving at her, and walked over to greet us. She wore the same blue scrubs as the other nurses and medical assistants. A stethoscope hung around her neck, and she was carrying my patient chart. Her name tag read Emma and had a smiley face on it.

"Hi, my name is Emma. I'll be preparing with you for your surgery in the upcoming weeks. Come with me." Emma led me and my parents from the waiting room and through a hallway filled with closed doors. After passing about five rooms, Emma stopped in front of one of the closed doors and turned the knob. The door opened on a bright exam room and Emma walked over to the exam table and patted it, smiling over at me as she did so. "Hop on, sweetie!"

I hopped on as my parents went to sit in the chairs just across from the exam table. Once we were all settled, Emma began to explain how the surgery procedure worked, breaking down the medical terms as we all listened intently.

"How long will the surgery take?" My father asked, pulling out a notepad from his pocket along with a pen to take notes, occasionally looking up and nodding. My mother, meanwhile, sat still with a straight face, taking in everything being said.

"About five hours and Mai will be asleep through all of it. She'll wake up sometime after the surgery is over in a recovery room, and then she'll stay about a week to recover."

My father raised his hand slightly and asked about the side effects of the surgery. I felt edgy in my seat, shaking a bit. My mother saw me and stood up, walking over to stand next to me and hold my hand for support. I buried my head in her chest like I did when I was six years old. Reality set in as I realized my life was about to change. I was about to have my first surgery in a few weeks and I was only ten years old. It felt like I had been through so much in my young life. The fear came and went and then subsided as I settled in to embrace my new hurdle. Or perhaps this was a new beginning.

***

Three weeks after my pre-surgery appointment, it was time for me to return to the hospital for my actual surgery appointment. Since I was supposed to be there for a week, I had to pack some things to get me through the week. My siblings helped me. Như was the first person to wish me luck. She stepped out of her room, hair tied up in a messy bun to keep it out of her face, and hugged me tightly while she kissed me all over. Minh, who was normally distant and didn't talk to me much, gave me a hug in his sweaty basketball uniform.

"Ew, Minh, did you shower?" I asked, grimacing while trying to keep in my disgust.

"Sorry, sis. I just came in from the backyard. Break a leg in that operation room, okay? You got this. I'll pray for you." He gave me a half-smile and then disappeared to the bathroom. Linh, Hồng-an, and Liên drew pictures of flowers and smiley faces for me to take to the hospital to help raise my spirits.

"Here you go. This is from all of us to keep you entertained. You can hang these up when you're in recovery," Linh exclaimed eagerly. My sisters gave me a tight hug before letting me go.

"Ready to go?" my father asked, reaching over to grab the keys on the kitchen table.

"Yes, Dad." My palms were sweaty and I shook a little inside.

"It's okay, you got this. Mom and your siblings and I are here for you," my father reassured me.

"Right, Mai, you're only ten years old, but we have great aspirations and plans for you. Remember how you couldn't walk when you were six? You cried out in agony every time Anne stretched your legs or when you were frustrated. You couldn't help but lash out and then beg me to take you home early. I was so mad at you, I thought you deserved to be grounded and scolded until you kicked that bad habit of yours. But you did it!"

"Yes, Mom," I nodded, still holding in my lingering feelings of worry. I gave her a half smile and scrunched up my chin to show my confidence. Deep down, I felt scared of what was to come.

My parents and I walked out to the car and once again, I felt the butterflies in my stomach and tried to distract myself with happier thoughts. I snapped myself back to the present as my father nudged me. My mother stood behind us, holding my bag of clothes and paperwork already signed. The engine roared and we were on our way. In the car, I remained silent, occasionally pulling on my hair while leaning on my mother's shoulder, as she had chosen to sit in the backseat with me for comfort.

"Don't pull on your hair; you're going to ruin it," my mother softly reminded me. I dropped my hand immediately from my hair and closed my eyes. The rumbling of the cars running in traffic died away as I slipped into a nap.

A little while later, we arrived at the hospital, checked in, and waited until my name was called. A medical assistant dressed in floral scrubs came out to greet us and lead us back to my hospital room.

"Right this way, please." We walked down the corridor to the recovery room and my parents put down my bag of clothes. Another nurse came in and took over.

If you need help, let us know," the nurse said as she handed me my hospital gown. She stepped out of the room to let me have a moment with my parents. I walked into the bathroom to change to my blue gown. I stepped out a moment later to see my parents waiting for me in front of the door.

"You look nervous, Mai," my mother mentioned. My father came behind my mother and nudged her, reminding her to let me have my space.

"I am." I walked toward the bed slowly and climbed up.

My parents leaned over and whispered words of encouragement in my ear. I nodded. I looked at my parents, one on each side of the bed.

"Mom?"

"Yes, Mai?"

"I love you."

"I love you, too," she said firmly. My father gave me a pat on the back. Then the nurse returned to get me ready. My parents followed behind her as she wheeled me out toward surgery and then waved to me before going back to the waiting room.

"Long time no see, Mai. Are you ready?" Dr. Georgeson greeted me behind his mask. He was dressed in a blue gown and scrubs.

"Ready as I'll ever be," I responded with a smile.

***

I woke up in a daze in the recovery room five hours later, and my parents were nowhere to be found. The nurse on duty happened to be in the room though and noticed I was awake.

"You're up! Would you like some water?"

"Yes, please." I couldn't move or turn because of the heavy casts on my legs, and I still felt drowsy from the anesthesia. I lifted my blankets to check out my legs and saw the casts went all the way up to my knees, and there was a wooden stick placed between my casts to keep my legs parallel to each other.

I set my blankets back over my legs and tried not think of how heavy the casts felt while I waited for the nurse to come back with water. When she returned, she handed me the glass of water with a warm smile, but I couldn't bring myself to return it. "Can I tell you something?" I asked her.

"Yes, Mai?"

"Please don't tell my parents."

"If it's not something harmful, I will do my best to keep it confidential." The nurse held my hand for reassurance.

"Well, um..." I lowered my voice a bit, trying to hold back tears.

"What is it, dear?"

"I hate having cerebral palsy!" I blurted out. "I've always wondered what it is like to walk normally like everyone else, you know? I was born this way, but no one would ever tell me what caused my condition." The dam of my repressed emotions broke.

"That must be so hard, Mai," the nurse said with a look of sympathy.

"Yeah," I blubbered out, in full straight tears now. The nurse held my hand and asked if she could give me a hug. I nodded. A while later, I felt my eyes drooping and the nurse smiled at me softly.

"It's all right, Mai. Get some sleep and I'm sure you'll feel better when you wake up." I nodded my head slightly and found myself easily drifting back off to sleep.

While sleeping, I had a dream.

In my dream, I saw myself in the future, older and healthier. I was sitting at a table smiling happily as I journaled in a notebook, writing on page after page. Suddenly my mother was in my room, standing over me and looking on as I wrote.

"Mai?"

I jumped, startled by her presence.

"Oh my god, Mom! You should have knocked!"

"What's with this attitude? I did not give birth to you just so you can speak to me in that tone. Where's the respect? You're such a child!" she scolded me harshly.

"Mom! No! Stop telling me I'm a child. Why don't you tell that to my siblings?" I asked angrily. She ignored my comment, her gaze falling onto my journal instead.

"And what's this?" She picked up my journal and stared at it for a long moment.

"Mom, that's my personal notebook! Give it back!" I ordered, reaching for it. My mother turned her hard gaze on me and I winced, knowing she was about to yell at me for being so rude. Instead, she slammed my journal back down onto the desk hard, huffed in anger, and stormed out of my room without another word. I watched her go before returning my attention back to my notebook. I picked it up, ready to return to writing but gasping in shock and sadness when I opened it up again. Everything I had written in it was gone! The pages were all blank, and I suddenly felt so defeated I wanted to cry.

"Mai? Mai? Wake up. It's time to eat lunch." I woke suddenly, dazed and a little disoriented. It took me a moment to realize I'd been dreaming and my parents were sitting next to my bed staring at me. My father held a tray of food in his hands, and after I pulled myself up to a sitting position, he placed it down in front of me. I stared at my food which consisted of a small salad, a tuna sandwich, some juice, a jello cup, and a yogurt. "Eat up, kiddo," my father said.

I ate, trying hard not to look directly at my mother after the terrible dream I had just had about her, afraid she would somehow find out about it. After I ate, I chatted with my parents for a bit, trying to shake off the dream but finding I still couldn't really look at my mother. I felt guilty for some reason. I decided I didn't really want to talk anymore and faked still being tired. My parents helped me to settle back into the bed and I laid back, closing my eyes. They waited for a little while to make sure I was asleep before they began to whisper among themselves about me and my future, unaware I was actually awake and could still hear them. I tried to tune them out because I didn't want to hear them talking about me, and soon enough, I fell asleep again for real.

A week later, on a sunny Friday morning, I was discharged. As I sat up in bed, I felt the pain from my legs pressing on my nerves. I closed my eyes and breathed deeply to distract myself. This was going to be a long recovery.

"You are all good to go," Dr. Georgeson said to my parents while they helped me gather my belongings and help me onto the wheelchair. My dad lifted the leg rest up so my casts could be supported. On my way out, I saw all the nurses who had been taking care of me in recovery waving at me and cheering me on. My parents wheeled me out to the car, helped me in, and we drove home.

***

After my surgery, my mother developed a routine of checking on me to see if I was in pain and then giving me morphine to relieve it. She also worked with me on the sitting and stretching exercises I had been instructed to do at home. Other times, Như would come and take over helping me whenever Mom was busy.

In the living room, I completed my stretching exercises along with Như guiding me. At times, she would watch me and then demonstrate so I could follow along. I grimaced, grunted, and pushed myself. Sweat ran down my face while I huffed and puffed.

"C'mon, stretch, Mai. Move your leg all the way up!" Như said, encouraging me. She raised my foot slightly while I sat against the wall counting to ten for each set.

"It hurts so much, Như. Sometimes I wonder what it's like not to have cerebral palsy," I lamented.

"Oh, sis. I know it's difficult, but you have to keep going so your legs get stronger."

"How much more do I have to do? It feels like years. I just… I can't… Why am I this way? A girl with cerebral palsy?" I pressed, trying to hold back this feeling of desolation.

"God loves you, sis. That's why He made you strong in spirit. He shined the light on you the day you were born," Như responded, leaning forward to embrace me.

"How do you know that?" I questioned, pressing her further.

"Because you're a fighter, and you don't give up," Như responded, tickling my cheeks.

"Oh, thanks," I mumbled, feeling my face turning red. A moment later, Minh came in from the kitchen with a bowl of oranges.

"Mom said to bring you two these," he huffed, handing the bowl to Như and me.

"Thanks, Minh. Come help Mai complete her last set of exercises," Như said, waving him over.

"I'm busy. Ask Liên, Linh, or Hồng-an," Minh retorted, feeling annoyed.

"Why don't you try and be a considerate brother?" Như sighed exasperatedly. Minh shrugged and wandered off before Như could ask him any more questions. She glared after him for a bit and then turned back to me, continuing her observations of my exercise routine.

Liên came down the stairs after hearing the commotion.

"Just let him be, Như. I'll help Mai," she offered.

"No, it's fine. I think I need a break." I placed my hands hard on the floor and lifted my head up, pressing down to stand up by myself.

"You got it, Mai?" Như asked, offering her arm to help me in case I fell.

"Yeah, I think I'm fine. Thanks for helping me exercise today," I said, feeling relieved the session was over.

"Careful. Walk slowly so you don't trip over, Mai," Liên said, looking on behind me. She turned and grabbed the walker near the stairs, walking it over to me.

"I am fine. Don't worry. I think you all are turning into our mother. Also, I don't like that walker. It creaks on the floor every time I use it." I pushed the walker aside.

"But you are still in the early stages of your recovery! Not using it might backfire on all the effort you and the doctor did to help regain your mobility," Như reasoned, pushing the walker back toward me.

"Fine," I said, heaving a big sigh. I had given into Như's request, but my heart was still set on the desire to walk on my own.

"You're fine. Using a walker is not a sign of weakness. It should be a badge of honor to your persistence. You can do this. There are so many more hurdles in life, but we believe in you," Liên responded.

"Thanks, guys," I said, my mouth curving into a slight grin. Maybe they were right. Maybe this was all just temporary and if I worked hard enough, I would be able to overcome any hurdle and achieve my own desires.

CHAPTER 5

NOT YOUR TYPICAL MATH STUDENT

―――

When I was in eighth grade, Algebra One was not my favorite class, nor was it a subject I was particularly good at. My face would break out in a sweat every time my teacher, Mr. Peterson, gave the class a math quiz.

"Class, math quiz time!" Mr. Peterson shouted in excitement as he hugged an armful of blank quizzes and walked down rows of desks to pass them out.

"Oh man," I muttered in defeat. I put my head down on my desk and pulled my blue hoodie over myself.

I was the only student in the whole class who walked with a walker. In addition to that, I also processed information a little bit differently than my friends. Cerebral palsy affected not just physical mobility, but also how my brain worked.

"Do your best, Mai. You'll be fine," Mr. Peterson reassured me, glancing at me momentarily before walking back over to his desk to set a timer. I sat working through the math quiz until I got to the last question. A few minutes later, I heard, "Time's up, class!" I was more than relieved to hear those words. We moved on to the next part of the lesson, listening to Mr. Peterson's monotone lectures about equations. After that, we completed worksheets at our desks independently while he graded our quizzes.

I dozed off to the sounds of pencils scratching along paper and the next thing I knew, Mr. Peterson was tapping my shoulder as he walked by my desk. Putting my math quiz face down in front of me, he "tsked" at me for having dozed off. My hands were shaking as I turned the paper over, and I was greeted with a bright-red C scrawled across the top of the quiz. I heaved a big sigh and bent down to retrieve my binder. I felt a poke from behind on my back.

"Hey, you dropped your pencil. Do you need help?" a girl about my age asked. She wore a shirt that said: *born to read numbers.* "My name's Tanya. I just came to this school. I noticed you have a walker. Let me know if you need anything."

"Thanks," I stammered, blushing red. "I am Mai." I was shocked because this was one of the first times someone, other than my siblings, was willing to acknowledge me.

"Is that the math quiz? How did you do?" Tanya asked, trying to ease into the conversation with me.

"Not very good. I got a C on it," I said, frowning in disappointment.

"That's tough," Tanya sympathized, her face scrunching. She reached over and gave me an encouraging handshake.

"I wanted an A, but this test was tricky. Now my mom will scold me like she always does if I get anything less than an A," I sighed loudly. "Math and I are not on great terms. It's like a bad relationship."

I thought about how much I despised math. I hated it even more because I did not fit the stereotypical Asian image of being smart and good at math, and I certainly wasn't fitting the model student image like my mother wanted.

"Oh, I'm sorry to hear that. I can help you if you want. Math is my favorite subject, and I have solid A's," Tanya responded, eager to help me.

I laughed nervously, thought about her offer, and nodded. "Thanks, Tanya. Now I have to figure out how to deal with my mother lecturing me tonight about this grade."

"I wish you luck," Tanya said, giving me a supportive smile.

***

When I got home from school, I walked slowly upstairs, holding on to the rails to keep myself from falling. When I finally made it up, the first thing I did was drop my backpack in my room before going to the bathroom to wash my face; I needed to clear away the disappointment of today's math test. I turned on the faucet, running my hand under the warm water for a moment before splashing some over my face. I looked up from the sink and stared at my reflection in the mirror, wondering how I would be able to handle telling my mother about my C grade. I pushed the thought away as I walked back to my room, unzipped my backpack, and retrieved my purple binder.

I pulled the chair from my desk and quickly sat down. I sat up straight and sharpened my pencil as I opened my binder and flipped to the Algebra One tab; the numbers in my math equations seeming to jump out at me as I stared at them. I scratched my head, trying to solve the word problems. To my disappointment, my brain wasn't cooperating with me.

I stood up and walked over to Như's room and knocked on her door. "Như?" I called out. When she didn't answer, I skipped over to Minh's room, then Hồng-an's, then Liên, and finally Linh; perhaps, they were all busy. I strolled back to my room, grabbed my assignment, and went downstairs.

I found my mother in the kitchen, bent over in her white, stained apron, stirring something in a large pot. The pot bubbled over as I moved near her and got a whiff of the cooking food. "Oh, Mom, watcha cookin'?" She turned to me with her tired face, left hand hanging over her forehead from the heat of the stove.

"How did you do on that math test?"

"Mom, how did you—" I stammered, taken aback by her intuition; I hadn't told her about today's math test.

"Did you forget I keep track of all your school schedules?" She reminded me in her typical tiger mom voice. "I'm making soup. What do you need?"

"Can you help me with math?" I wondered.

My mother turned to me. "Come sit at the table. I'll be right there." I sat and waited as she turned off the stove and strolled over to me.

I felt chills running down my back.

She explained it to me while I sat there on the dining room table scratching my head. She explained it like she expected me to know the answers.

Then my mother excused herself to run upstairs and grab a whiteboard. She came downstairs a moment later with it in her hands and proceeded to write some numbers and explain again how to solve the word problems. I sat there quietly, my lips quivering in nervousness.

"Mom, I still don't get it," I whined.

"That's why you need to pay attention more when I am explaining," she chastised me, shaking her finger in my direction.

"Mom, it's not even that. It's just that math is too hard!"

"Well, your father and I were the best math students in our classes. Why aren't you? We come from the same family and have the same genes. If you can get through math, you're smart! You can do it!"

"Mom, why does being good at math have to be associated with being smart? I don't get it!" I complained, close to tears now.

"We just want you to have a stable future, and you'll get that with a good job in the medical field, like a pharmacist or doctor!"

"What if I don't want to be either of those? I like writing; maybe I could be a writer?" I replied hopefully. My mother scoffed at me.

"Go into writing? How much does a writer even make? That's not a real job." I glared at her, upset she wouldn't see it from my perspective. My mother leaned back in her chair. Crossing her arms, she looked at me straight in the eye as she spoke. "The world is full of possibilities, Mai." I stared at her for a moment, perplexed that she did not try to understand my perspective but discouraged me.

"Mom, you're confusing! If the world is full of possibilities, why am I not allowed to be what I want to be?"

"You just don't get it, do you? Being in the healthcare field is a noble career. Family pride. You know how many people would be so proud if that is your profession?"

"Oh, Mom. What am I going to do with you? When will I ever be able to make my own choices?" I sighed in exasperation.

"As long as you're in this house, you will adhere to our rules, understand?" my mother pressed. "Besides, you're capable of doing it if you try hard enough."

I paused, sitting in silence, knowing we didn't see eye to eye. I frowned, debating between whether to show her my math quiz now or wait until later. I decided to go for it.

"Mom? I, uh…" I could feel myself starting to hyperventilate. I turned the other way and grabbed my backpack, retrieving the math quiz from the inside and holding it to my chest. My mother raised her eyebrows.

"Hm, Mai?"

"I, uh…" My face turned red as I felt close to tears. With my hand shaking, I handed her my math quiz. She took it from me and stared at the bright-red C. Her face tensed and then she turned to me, giving me *the look*.

"How'd you get a C? Did you not study? Did your sister not help you?" She stopped and held her breath to avoid lecturing me as she glanced briefly at the doorway leading out of the kitchen. The door was ajar, and I realized she was worried about Như overhearing while she was trying to study.

"No, but I tried to understand it though! Please, please, please, don't be mad at me," I pleaded, holding on to her arms. She took a breath and let it out slowly, calming herself.

"I am not angry; I am disappointed. At this rate, you're not on track toward any health career," she sighed, staring at my math quiz once again. I stared at her, not surprised in the least that she had brought up the health career thing again. I wanted to tell her to give me a break, but I knew that would never happen.

"Mom, is there anything you would want me to be besides a pharmacist or doctor? Geez, you're so short-sighted!"

This triggered her.

"I can't believe you didn't study hard enough! A C is bad!" she scolded, her eyes raising in anger.

"Mom! Just listen to me! A C grade does not mean I am failing! Besides, I am still in middle school! Pharmacy school is way in the future!" I shouted back, close to my breaking point. "You know what? I'm tired. I'm done!" I grabbed up my things from the kitchen table quickly and stormed out, heading back to my room as quickly as my legs would let me go. I heard my mother huffing in the kitchen after me and complaining about how ungrateful I was, but I ignored her ranting.

Once I reached my room, I threw my stuff on my desk and shut myself in, wishing I had never told my mother about my quiz. I longed for my feelings to be validated and heard by my mother. All my friends were telling me how they were close to their parents and siblings, and I wanted that same relationship.

My mother seemed absolutely set on my career being in the medical field, and the more she pushed it, the more I pushed back. It was just another thing we didn't see eye to eye on, keeping our relationship strained. In secret, I allowed myself to cry and sit with my feelings. I closed my eyes, remembering how far I had to come to get to this point in my life.

I thought about how both my parents were immigrants and how they had been through a lot in their life. They had left Vietnam because of war, and then spent their life here in America working long hours to provide for their family. They had experienced trauma, and one of the ways they dealt with the pain of their trauma was by raising trophy children. Trophy children were supposed to listen to their parents' perspectives, do well in school, seldom argue, never talk back or question their parents' authority, and pursue the life their parents deemed suitable.

I was definitely not a trophy child. Not like my other siblings, who seemed to be so obedient and smart and never disagreed with our parents about their futures. I sat with my anger and hurt for a few minutes before there was a knock on my door.

"Mai?"

"I am not coming out!" I said, sniffing back angry tears.

"It's me, Như. Can I come in?"

"Only if you agree not to snitch on me to Mom and Dad," I said, getting off my bed and heading for the door. I gripped the door handle as I waited for her reply.

"Okay." I heard her say softly. I opened the door slowly and Như looked at me with sympathetic eyes. "Mai, listen. I overheard you and Mom arguing; she only wants the best for us, so sometimes she'll be that way, you know?"

"I don't understand. How am I wrong when I was just trying to explain myself to her? Mom didn't even give me a chance to really explain," I lamented.

"Well, I think it's because when you spoke in a very rude tone, that's a sign of disrespect. I know how hard it is for you to accept."

"Accept? I wish Mom would be a lot easier on me." I looked the other way, not facing my sister, wishing there was somehow a magic solution to my mother's tough love.

"Right, I know. Mom wasn't easy on me either. But I want you to know she didn't mean it. It was just how she was brought up, and I know she just wants the best life for you. She thinks you show her your respect by not complaining and doing what she wants," Như explained, gesturing with her hands.

"She didn't even care about my feelings," I shot back at Như, frowning. I moved to sit down on my bed, tracing the patterns on the bedspread with my hand.

Như came over and sat next to me, putting her hand on my shoulder. "No, it's not that. How do I put this in simple words? It's the Asian mama's way of showing love."

"Well, I prefer the American way of love," I quipped. Như sighed, burying her face in her hands. Her head shook slightly.

"What am I going to do with you?"

"What do you mean, what are you going with me? You're supposed to say you're going to be here for me." My voice got really low. I wanted to reach out to Như and tell her how much I appreciated her trying to connect with me, but I wasn't comfortable hugging her at the moment.

"I love you, Mai. So does Minh, Linh, Hồng-an, and Liên."

"Thanks. I appreciate that. It's just I don't know. I am not ready to talk to Mom about what I really want to do. I don't think she will listen anyway. She'll just get upset with me again."

"Just take your time. There's no rush. This is your time to reflect." Như got up and closed the door behind her. I thought about what she said and realized she had done her best to try and comfort me.

As I gathered my thoughts, Hồng-an and Linh came into my room and sat with me, holding my hands on either side of me.

"Hey, I know Mom has been hard on you, but just know I'm here, okay?" Hồng-an said, wrapping her arms around me in a warm hug. Linh got up to light a candle and turn off the lights in my bedroom.

"Let's pray," Linh said, turning to look at me.

"Okay," I nodded, starting to feel better.

"Hail Mary, full of grace," we began the prayer in unison.

After praying, my sisters left my room to give me some space and I decided to take out my journal and write.

> *Dear Lord,*
> *When will this be over? When will my mother relax and trust me? Help me prove myself. Help me prove that even in the face of hardships, I have the courage to do what I love, not only for my own happiness but so I can be at my full potential and at your full brightness shining upon me.*
> *Amen*

I longed to be a writer one day, traveling the world and exploring new places like London, Paris, and Italy. But Mom wanted me to go into the medical field for economic reasons. I wasn't ready to face my mother and tell her the truth about my own plans for my future.

I closed my journal once again and moved on to completing the rest of my homework assignments.

I stayed up until midnight doing homework.

I moved to sit down on the edge of my bed, crossing my legs at the ankle and staring intently at the Blessed Mother statue that sat on a shelf by the door. I'd been wrestling with my feelings for too long. Slowly, I let my tears flow again. I cupped my hands over my face, closed my eyes and saw nothing but darkness.

The noise coming from my throat spoke to the pain in my soul. The sound was similar to a bunch of horses galloping away and leaving nothing behind but a trail of sand.

CHAPTER 6
EMERGENCE

Eighth grade was a time of self-discovery. I had overcome a surgery three years prior, enabling me to walk a little bit better on my own. This milestone was significant because it signified my physical independence and confidence. The medical research and possibilities gave me and my family hope. I was also gaining new skills and friends in school.

Each day, I made progress walking around campus, but I still felt self-conscious when I saw other students around me run, jump, or climb stairs. I always found myself trying to catch up with others, but was often lagging behind instead. Even though I felt exhausted at times, I knew this temporary pain would come to pass. I learned to deal with and push past with the physical pain I endured, understanding that by dealing with it now and trying my best, I would eventually enjoy better mobility and more independence later on.

An hour passed by quickly as my classmates and I sat listening to our teacher, Mrs. McGinn, teaching us about grammar and storytelling. It had been a long day at school and I was exhausted. I struggled to keep my head up when the bell rang to signal the end of class. I stood up to put my backpack on with the other students. Mrs. McGinn waved at me as I put my binder in my backpack and scooted out of my chair.

"Bye, Mai!" she called out to me. I waved back to her with a tired smile as I headed toward the door to retrieve my rickety, silver walker from the corner of the classroom.

"Bye! Thank you!" I said as I grabbed hold of my walker and walked out.

"Mai!" I heard Tanya call me as I walked across campus. I caught sight of her and noticed she wore a purple shirt with flashy overalls and Converse shoes.

"Tanya!" I shouted, waving at her. I pressed harder against my walker, pushing it forward. The wheels creaked on the concrete as I pushed, causing me to look down instead of focusing on where I was walking. Suddenly, I was brought to a stop when my walker hit a tree just off the path. The impact was enough to cause my grip on the walker to loosen and I could feel myself falling as if in slow motion.

Thump. I landed flat on the ground. "Ow..." I let out a groan and struggled to get up. "Geez, not again," I muttered, feeling frustrated with myself. Tanya stood behind me, her mouth hanging open.

"What happened? Are you okay?" She extended her arms out to help me up.

"Thanks, Tanya," I stammered, blushing. I gripped my walker tighter. "I'm fine, no need to worry. I'm okay, girl."

"You sure? This is the first time I have seen you fall." Tanya stepped back to give me some space.

"Yeah, I'm sure." We continued walking together toward the pick-up zone in the parking lot. I stood next to her while I waited for Như to come pick me up.

"Um... Do you mind if I ask you a question?" Tanya hesitated, making eye contact with me.

"Hm?" I shifted my attention to her, rolling my shoulders to keep my backpack from slipping off.

"Were you born like that?" She glanced at my legs briefly and put her hand on my shoulder to show support.

"Yeah, I was diagnosed with cerebral palsy when I was a toddler."

Tanya nodded. She thought for a while and then asked, "Is it hard for you to walk?"

"Well, I was born early, at like twenty-eight weeks, and when I was about a year old, my parents noticed I wasn't meeting my milestones. They took me to a doctor who put me in a therapy program, and a few years ago I had to go through surgery," I said, letting myself be vulnerable.

"Does it hurt?" Tanya wondered out of curiosity. She shuffled her feet nervously.

"Not really. I'm used to walking this way. It's just how I am," I said, pausing to wipe a small tear that had escaped my eyes.

Tanya reached out to me. "You're crying? Why?" She then pulled a tissue from her bag. "Here, take this." I took the tissue from her as Tanya then motioned for me to follow her and we walked over to a nearby bench, close to the school's front gate.

"No, it's fine. I mean—it's just, no one ever asked me what it's like to have a disability. I've felt so alone my whole life even though I am surrounded by people," I blurted out.

"I know that feeling all too well. If you ever need help, Mai, let me know what I can do. Wanna come to my house later so we can talk?" Tanya asked with a hopeful look on her face. I paused for a bit, deciding I could trust Tanya with my story. After all, she had reached out to me on that first day of school in algebra class.

"I wish. My mom won't let me go anywhere after school unless it's school related."

"Oh, that's a bummer," Tanya said as I looked on to watch for my sister's car pulling up in the parking lot.

"It is. My mom is strict about who I hang out with and what I can do. I rarely have anyone over to my house or go to anyone's house because my mom wants me to study hard all the time. So the only time I actually get to hang out with friends is at school." I frowned and shrugged my shoulders. I heard a honk and looked up to see Nhu's car pulling up. "I gotta go, Tanya." Tanya nodded and waved as she watched me walk over and get into my sister's car. I waved back at her through the window as Nhu began to drive away.

"Who was that, sis?" Nhu asked.

"I made a new friend, and her name is Tanya. She seems really nice," I said, hugging my backpack tighter on my lap.

"That's really nice, Mai," Nhu replied, her gaze focused on the road.

"Yeah," I said, pausing for a long time. I didn't want to tell her anything more as I was trying to embrace this new friendship.

As soon as we got home and Nhu parked the car, she turned to face me. "You seem quiet today, sis. Are you okay?"

I broke into a slight smile. "I'm okay. Today I told my friend about my disability. She understood me."

"Looks like you two were meant to meet. I am proud of you; I know how hard it is for you to open up." Nhu leaned over to embrace me.

"Thanks, sis. Yeah, God was here all along." I pulled out of her embrace, turning to let myself out of her car. Nhu turned off the car engine and walked inside the house with me. As we stepped inside the house, my father was waiting for me at the kitchen table. She and I both took off our shoes, and then she retreated up the stairs.

"How was school today?" my father asked, eager to hear about my day. He glanced down and smoothed over his shirt, and then he pulled out two chairs, inviting me to sit down with him. "Come sit, Mai." I was taken aback by his gesture of support. My father, a quiet man of few words, was making an effort to reach out to me.

"School was okay. It was a little better than yesterday," I responded.

"That's good to hear, Mai. Keep it up," he replied encouragingly.

"Thanks," I mumbled uneasily.

"You're welcome, Mai." Dad patted me on the back and gave me a side hug. He clasped my hands in both of his for support.

"Dad? What's up with you today?" It was unusual for my father to be overly affectionate with hugs like this. I held myself back from being too happy; this was a bit unreal. I was not used to much physical affection from either of my parents. I was used to my parents ignoring me whenever I asked questions or shooing me away when they were in the middle of something.

"I have been reading some writing of yours." My father gestured excitedly.

"My writing?" I was confused; I hadn't shared any of my writing with my parents.

"Yes, in your room," he explained.

"What? Dad! You looked at my personal writing?" I looked at him in shock, both annoyed that he had gone through my stuff but also curious as to why all of a sudden he would take an interest in my passion.

"Was I being snoopy?"

"Yeah, you were!" I shouted all of a sudden. I didn't want my parents to discover I was writing. "I thought you would be mad at me..." It was strange to me that he seemed more excited than angry. "Didn't you both say I can't be a writer? That I need to persevere and become a pharmacist?" I asked again, confused.

I heard footsteps of my mother coming downstairs from the kitchen before my father could answer my question. She responded loudly, "Hung, don't start giving her ideas. She has to work hard to stay on track and become a pharmacist."

"I knew this was going to happen," I moaned, disappointed.

"Her writing's actually pretty good. You should read it when you have an opportunity," my father explained to my mother, gently reprimanding her.

"Look, she has cerebral palsy and she has her whole life ahead of her. Who's going to take care of her when we're old? She needs a stable career, and she can't be scribbling words in class when she should be maintaining her 4.0 average to get into a great school," my mother said, her eyebrows raising and looking directly at him.

"I am going to my room. This is giving me a headache," I said, getting up from the table.

"Finish your homework and ask your sister to check it over after you're done," my mother called after me. An uneasy feeling crept over me as I walked up the stairs and I ended up storming into my room and slamming the door behind me.

"Mai, I heard that from down here! You know what the rules are! You are not allowed to slam doors in this house!" my mother hollered up the stairs. I could hear the frustration in her voice. I couldn't understand the need for my mother to be so strict with me. However, I knew if I wanted any chance of pursuing a writing career without her interfering, I'd have to prove to her that being a writer was an actual career. I wanted to be the best writer I could be.

I sat down at my desk and began writing instead of doing my homework. I glanced at the door to see if my mom was going to come bursting in, afraid she would discover me writing instead of working on my homework. The clock ticked away the time, and after about an hour of writing, I put away my journal and took out my homework.

There was a knock at the door a few minutes later. "Who's there?"

"It's me, Như. Can I come in?" she asked from behind the door.

"It's unlocked. You can come in." I turned back to my writing. Như opened the door and let herself in, sitting down on my bed. "I heard the conversation between Mom and Dad. Do you want to talk about it?"

I nodded and got up from my desk to join her on my bed. Như caressed my hair and embraced me. It was her soft touch that broke the dam. I couldn't hold it in anymore and I began to cry, letting my tears fall freely. "Hush, I'm right here, sis. It's okay." She went to my desk to grab me a tissue. I sat up and took the tissue from her, wiping off the tears before they fell to the ground.

"Thanks," I said, locking myself in her embrace. Như hugged me tightly, patting my back up and down. Still holding me in her arms, she said, "Hey, I'm sorry I haven't had a chance to spend time with you lately. I've just been so busy studying for my MCAT so I can get the best scores for medical school."

"You know, you've always been our parent's favorite. You're studying so hard to become a doctor and you always do what they say. How come Mom and Dad don't yell at you as much as they do me?" I questioned, finally releasing myself from her embrace.

Như rubbed my hair. "Oh, Mai, please don't say that. I am sure Mom and Dad love you just the same."

"That's not true, is it? They are a lot stricter with me than you," I replied, wiping off the last of my tears.

"You wanna know why they are a lot stricter with you?"

"Why, Như?"

"They're afraid they can't take care of you when they get old because you need more help with walking and day-to-day life." I stared at her for a long moment, processing this information. I hugged Như tighter as she said this. I confronted the thought of my parents getting old and felt this gnawing feeling creep up on me.

My sister continued. "They only want the best for you, but sometimes their expectations come down harder on you."

"I'm not a baby you know."

"Of course, I know you're not a baby. That's why I'm talking to you heart to heart right now. You gotta understand that our parents are from a different generation than us. They were immigrants, and they really dig that American dream," Như explained.

"I guess they really want me to make something of myself." I put my hands in my chin, deep in thought.

"That's right, but hey. Just work, do your best, and keep writing on the side. You have my full support, and even if you don't end up being a pharmacist, you'll be a writer."

"Như?"

"What, sis?"

"I am sorry for all the times I've never hung out with you. I knew you were busy, but I didn't know how busy you were. And I'm sorry if I annoyed you more times than I can count."

"I'm sorry as well for not being there as much as you would like me to. I should step it up and do my part as your older sister."

"Do you think Mom will eventually come around, you know, to me switching my interests? I honestly hate science and math," I whispered.

"Oh Mai, you're only thirteen. How can you be so worried at this age?"

"I was just asking," I said, feeling myself breathe faster.

"Well, I can't promise you she'll come around that quickly, but I can tell you that if you do your work, stay out of trouble at school, come home on time, and work hard, she'll leave you alone and we're all going to do our best to be there for you, deal?"

"Deal." We both linked our pinkies in a promise.

From then on, the conflicts with my parents eased up as I worked hard to follow what Như had said. I'd come home from school and put my best effort on my homework, which kept my mother happy. Now that I knew I had my sister's unwavering support, my confidence grew day by day. My new self was starting to emerge. It had been struggling to come out for a long time and I was finally starting to learn how to embrace it.

CHAPTER 7

FINDING MYSELF

I was in my freshman year of high school when I realized I was capable of making my own decisions. After two uneventful years of middle school, I transitioned to high school with more questions than answers. This rebellious stage was further complicated by the raging hormones in my body and the unappealing acne on my forehead. I resisted the urge to poke at my face while trying to deal with the occasional communication misunderstandings with my parents. For the most part, I got along well with my family, but could not help feeling moody at times.

Sunset High School was a school that was easy to get lost in because it was so big and had been built like a maze on the inside. There were gates surrounding the school and a couple of green benches outside. The school had a large open space and that made it easier for me to walk around with my walker.

On that first sunny day of fall, Như drove me to school along with my other siblings sitting in the backseat while I sat in the front. As we got closer to the parking lot of the school, my anxiety went up. My siblings sensed I was adjusting to a new school and did their best to calm me down.

"You got this, Mai!" they all said in unison as Như pulled into the parking lot a moment later.

"Thanks, y'all," I muttered nervously as I opened the car door, grabbed my backpack, and wriggled my arms through. Linh and Minh opened their side of the door to help get my walker from the trunk of the car. Như once again flashed me a smile and gave me a thumbs up. I turned to walk into my English Honors class, taking each step slowly to prevent myself from tripping over.

As I was getting to the classroom door to wait in line, I felt a poke from behind my back.

"Mai?" a voice called out. I turned around to see a familiar face.

"Tanya! I didn't know you were in this class too! Wow!" I lowered my voice and broke into a wide smile. The jitters of the first day of school eased as I settled comfortably into a conversation with my best friend. We hadn't seen each other all summer.

Tanya winked. "I was walking behind you the whole time, but I wanted it to be a surprise!"

A few moments later, a woman dressed in a white blouse and black skirt sprinted across to her classroom, keys dangling from her arm.

"Whew, made it! Hi, class, I'm Mrs. Webb. Please come in quietly and take your seats." Mrs. Webb opened the door wider as the class scurried in.

We walked in and took our seats while I placed my walker in the corner of the classroom and locked the wheels. As I scanned my surroundings, I could sense this English class would be a favorite of mine.

"Settle down." Mrs. Webb turned to the board and wrote out the day's agenda. She dusted off the chalk on her hands before continuing. "Okay class, today's lesson is on memoir writing. For this assignment, I will allow you to have some free reign. You will write a memoir essay about your life and turn the assignment in for a letter grade. The due date is three weeks from today."

Sighs and groans were heard as soon as Mrs. Webb finished giving her instructions. I secretly cheered inside as I knew this was my opportunity to write not only as a homework assignment, but also as a small escape from the reality that my strict mother somehow tried to inflict upon me to go into STEM fields.

I sat, listening attentively as Mrs. Webb discussed our lesson on reflective writing for the class period. The more I listened to her lectures, the more engrossed I became as she skillfully used analogies and metaphors to help my classmates and I understand the different styles of writing.

Before long, the lecture was over. I sat there for a few minutes in awe of this new teacher of mine. It was only day one and already I felt in my heart that I belonged in this space.

"Class is dismissed," Mrs. Webb finally said. I stood up from my desk and grabbed my backpack from my chair when I suddenly realized I could use this assignment to somehow convince my parents that no matter what, I wasn't going to let their words get in the way of my aspirations.

I walked over to the corner of the classroom, pushed the handle on my walker to unlock it, and went on my way. As I turned a corner toward the gate, I felt my legs shaking beneath me. I lost my balance and felt the gravity sway away from me as I struggled to keep my walker from twisting due to the steep curve of the path.

As I did, I felt a hand on my shoulder. "Whoa there! Are you okay?" I turned my head around to see Tanya standing behind me, her left hand on the handles of my walker and her right hand in the middle of my back. "I got you, girl. That was a really rough path right there."

She looked taller than me now, and much more mature and confident than when I had met her back in eighth grade. I looked at her and gave a tiny smile, hiding a fear of burdening inside my heart. I was used to my family watching over me, but Tanya gave me a different perception of care: the care of someone my own age.

Tanya and I continued walking down to the next class, which I unwillingly participated in. Out of all the six classes I had, math was a little more bearable because Tanya was in the same class as me, and English was a class I already enjoyed. Lunchtime rolled around, and I scurried off with my walker to find my best friend. I walked over to the cafeteria, stopped at the door, leaned over to keep my balance, and put my other hand on the handle to open it.

The other students walked in one by one after me. Tanya eventually found me as she walked in, and we sat next to each other, ate, and talked. After lunch, it was time for the last class of the day, Adapted PE, where a teacher who specialized in modified physical education came and worked with me.

Ms. Everson was my Adapted PE teacher who loved working with disabled students. The exercises were not easy, but I knew they were necessary for the strength of my legs. The class session brought me back to the memories of working with Jane and Anne when I was a kid. I huffed and puffed my way through the PE class, feeling my heart beating faster and faster.

When the bell rang to signal the end of class, relief washed over me as I waved goodbye to Ms. Everson.

"Have a great day! I'll see you tomorrow!" Ms. Everson waved back at me as I headed out the door of the gym. Tanya was already waiting for me when I got outside. We walked out together toward the gate to the parking lot to wait for my sister.

A few minutes later, I heard a honk as Minh's car pulled up to the gate.

"Bye, Tanya! Thanks for waiting with me," I called after her as she moved to the corner to walk home. I got into the car and pulled my seat belt over my shoulder. Once I was buckled, I looked at my brother with curiosity.

"Where's Như? Is she busy studying again?" I asked, feeling a wave of uneasiness coming on.

"Close the passenger door. C'mon, I've got no time. I'm already late to my meeting with my friends. I'll drop you off at home. And while you're at it, give Mom this." He handed me one of his dirty basketball uniforms. "Tell Mom to wash this for me when I drop you off."

I shifted uneasily in my seat. "Why don't you tell her yourself, or better yet, wash the uniform yourself, bro," I retorted. "Seriously, will you ever be a little considerate?" I looked away from him and stared straight ahead to the road. He shrugged my comments off and began to drive toward home, picking up speed as he went, until it felt like he was driving too fast. "Slow down bro! I'm dizzy!" I begged, gripping my hands together to prevent myself from slumping forward.

"It's fun. Loosen up a little bit, baby sis. You have your seat belt on already." He turned a corner and drove straight down to our neighborhood street. He stopped and parked the car in the driveway.

"Hurry, hurry! I'm late, Mai," Minh said as he unlocked the door for me. I wrinkled my nose and held his uniform, trying hard to hide my annoyance at his risk-taking nature.

"Fine, have fun with your friends, bro," I muttered awkwardly. Minh drove off before I could say another word, and I walked up to the door from the driveway. Letting myself in the house, I noticed that my body felt shaken up from the speed at which Minh drove his car. I figured out why he was the loose cannon of our family; he was always taking risks, never caring what other people thought of him. I heaved a long sigh, secretly wishing I could be more like him and enjoy that kind of freedom.

I walked upstairs to my room, shutting myself in and dropping my backpack on the bed. I sat still, my hands in my chin and deep in thought. My parents are people too, and I knew I could no longer hold myself back. I retrieved my backpack on the bed and pulled out my binder.

A while later, I walked over and knocked gently on Như's bedroom door. "Như?"

"The door is unlocked. Do you need something? I'm kinda busy," she said from behind her door.

"Um… I have this memoir assignment that's due in three weeks. Could I interview you? Is this a good time?" I asked reluctantly.

"Sure, I can spare a few minutes." She opened the door and stepped out. I motioned for her to come with me, and we walked over to my room to do the interview for the assignment. We got to my room and sat on my bed as I reached over to my desk to grab my yellow notepad.

"Okay, ready to start?" Như asked me. I nodded, marking the first bullet point on the pad.

"I'm ready when you are, sis," Như and I sat awhile as she told me the details about my life when I was little and what it had been like for her to take care of me and watching the family grow as well. Then she got to the part when my parents found out about my disability, her face taking on a look of consideration as she deliberated how to tell me the aftermath of dealing with me as a disabled sister in the family.

"Then we found out you had cerebral palsy and Mom was disappointed. But she eventually accepted it and got past the disappointment. She was also hard on all of us because she wanted us to know how to take care of you."

"Oh." I frowned, suddenly feeling a new guilt about how I judged my mother so harshly. As a growing teen just trying to figure herself out, I grappled with this nagging feeling once again. I knew the circumstances of my birth did not change my mother's concern for me. I realized my mother cared in the best way she knew how.

I struggled to find the common ground between the two of us as mother and daughter.

"Yes, she really loves you, Mai."

"Như, I'm sorry." I started to cry.

Như placed her arm on my shoulder, stopped me, and said, "There's no need to apologize. You're still learning about yourself and remember, I'm here for you." I reached over to the tissue box on my desk, pulled one out and dabbed at my eyes. As our conversation ended, there was a knock at the door.

"Như, Mai, it's dinner time!" said Hồng-an from behind the door.

"We're just about done! Give us two minutes," Như responded back. "Mai, you good?"

"I'm good. Thank you for helping me."

"Let's go to dinner."

"Yes." I held Như's hand and we walked downstairs to the kitchen.

Như and I sat down next to each other as everyone gathered around the table. Hồng-an, Liên, Minh, Linh, Mom, and Dad all held hands and we prayed.

"Bless this bounty of food we have, for our home, our safety, and our family, Lord, in the name of the Father, Son, and Holy Spirit. Amen," Dad said.

"Amen," I said.

"Amen," Mom said.

"Amen," all five of my siblings said in unison.

"Let's eat, kids. Update me on school," said Dad.

"I have this project that's due in three weeks. The assignment is to write about my life. I already interviewed Như. I am about to start after I am done with dinner."

"That's good. Remember to focus on school first so everything goes well after you graduate from college," said my mother. I felt she nagged me too much about school, and my fear of not being able to live up to her expectations irritated me. I wasn't ready for her to push this on me once again. It wasn't that I didn't care, but as a freshman trying to figure herself out, I needed to have some space to think and explore what I like and what I didn't like.

I shifted slightly in my seat, giving Như an anxious look. Liên looked at Hồng-an, who turned to look at Minh and Linh. Everyone got really quiet and didn't speak for the rest of the dinner. I was scared to death, and every part of my body felt chills all over. My mother always had a knack for knowing what was going on. I ate quickly, shoving the food into my mouth. As soon as I was finished, I excused myself and rushed upstairs to the safety of my room, closing the door behind me. I laid down on my bed, trying to calm my nerves. I laid there for a good half hour before I realized that working on my assignment would probably help take my mind off my sudden anxiety. I got up and went to retrieve my notes before sitting down at my desk and opening up my laptop. Once I was set up to write, I began to work on the assignment in earnest.

As my fingers danced up and down my laptop, all the time in the world seemed to stop as I engrossed myself in my assignment. A thought came up about the sacrifices my family made to give me a better life. What if my parents didn't come to America? I decided that no matter what, my story must be told.

I started the memoir off by talking about the difficulties my parents faced in moving to America from Vietnam, wanting to build a better life for themselves and our family. I blended this into talking about my life, the trials I had faced as a young girl, and the expectations that weighed on me from my parents, my family, and even my culture. I wrote about my struggle to follow my own dreams instead of my mother's, and how being a pharmacist was what she wanted for me, but not what I wanted.

It was close to midnight when I stopped writing. I checked my assignment to see if there were any missing details. Satisfied, I closed my laptop and walked over to my bed, falling under the blankets in a deep slumber.

***

The next morning, Như drove me to school. As I got into the car and buckled up, I asked her, "You guys were really quiet last night during dinner when Mom brought up the college conversation. What happened?"

Như breathed, smoothing over her jacket at the stoplight as I looked directly at her. I waited. "Um... It was an awkward subject. I didn't want to say anything that would trigger Mom, but I could see and feel your anxiety."

"Oh, did you know something was up? I am not ready for that conversation." I frowned. I wanted to tell Như, but the more I thought about it, the more I knew I wasn't ready.

"Well, I know how Mom is. She's just a tough, no-nonsense, facts-and-logic kind of mother. She's also a workaholic," Như reasoned, concentrating on the road ahead. "Let's talk about something else. No need to stress over that."

I tensed in my seat. "But I am still frustrated with Mom. She's being unreasonable."

"Right," Như responded, turning a corner and driving into the school's parking lot.

"I wished you could have said something to Mom," I said, unbuckling myself. "I gotta go, but we can talk more about it when you come pick me up."

"Have a great day at school, Mai. I'll see you later." Như opened her driver side door, helped me get my walker from her car's trunk, gave me a quick hug, and went back into her car.

"Bye, sis. Love you!" I waved at her from. She blew me a kiss and then went on her way.

My day was just getting started and I whispered to myself, "Please let this be a good day."

CHAPTER 8

DELIBERATION

I walked to my English classroom slowly, gripping the red handles of my walker, where I was greeted by Mrs. Webb and the whole class. Everyone's faces were tired from the early time of the class, but I was excited to get the day started. I heaved a big sigh of relief before taking my seat.

"Class, today we are going to learn about how to start your memoir essay. Did anyone interview your parents or find anyone to interview yet?" Mrs. Webb said, turning to the board to write the agenda.

 Everyone was eerily quiet and didn't raise their hands except for me and Tanya.

"Wow, there's only two of you? What happened to the rest of you?"

"Mrs. Webb, I'm done with the assignment," I announced proudly. A round of groans followed my announcement. Mrs. Webb turned around, shushing the class.

"Settle down, class. Mai, may I see you after class?" Mrs. Webb glanced briefly at me.

"Yes, Mrs. Webb." I nodded anxiously. Was I in trouble? I went back to paying attention to her lesson, pushing the thought away.

"Can anyone tell me what their best childhood memory is?" she asked the class.

I raised my hand in the air with a tiny smile on my face. "What's one of them, Mai?" Mrs. Webb called on me, her finger pointing toward me.

"The best memory I have ever had was when my sisters helped me with my exercises," I answered excitedly.

"Good job, Mai! My most memorable moment was when I graduated from college and got hired as a teacher. I enjoyed teaching, and you all are the reason I do what I do," Mrs. Webb responded, her radiant smile visibly present on her face.

She eventually called on another student to answer her question, and then continued her lecture on showing us how to write the memoirs, walking up and down the rows of desks to make sure we were on task. I listened to her despite having already completed my memoir the night before.

Then she said, "Keep working on that memoir assignment. Class is dismissed." As my classmates headed out the door, Mrs. Webb turned to the board and wiped off her notes.

I stayed behind to wait. Mrs. Webb went over to her desk to grab her folder and grade book. She gestured for me to come toward her.

"Mai, how did you complete that assignment so quickly? I gave everyone else three weeks to complete the project, yet it only took you a night to complete it?" She moved her graded assignments aside to give me space on her desk as I put my backpack down.

"Yes. I finished it right away because I had a lot on my mind. So I took that chance to write about me," I responded, fiddling my fingers nervously.

"May I see the assignment?" Mrs. Webb asked.

"Sure, Mrs. Webb." I retrieved my laptop from my backpack and showed her my complete memoir essay. I watched as she read my story and I could see her eyes brimming with tears.

"Wow, this is awesome, Mai. Your family went through a lot to get through the hard times." I got really quiet. My lips turned upside down and, finally, I couldn't hold it in anymore. I cried, looking down to see tears already making their way down to my pink blouse.

"What's wrong, Mai?" Mrs. Webb gave me an empathetic look.

"I actually had to write this in secret. The assignment was my way of letting myself deal with my feelings." I finally found a new understanding as I opened myself up to my teacher. The understanding that I couldn't find with my parents when it came to encouraging me to pursue my passion. In conversing with Mrs. Webb, I found a safe space to talk. As a student with cerebral palsy, it helped to know I had a trusting adult who believed in me.

"I can see that. You should always follow your heart, dear. No one can tell you what you cannot do. You have to persist and keep going. Don't give up," Mrs. Webb said, handing me a tissue.

"My parents don't want me to pursue the arts." I felt the tears falling again.

Mrs. Webb looked at me with sympathy. "Oh, why is that?" She pushed the tissue box to me once more, fully this time as she listened intently to my feelings.

"They think being a writer is a waste of time, especially my mother." I sat up straighter this time, grateful for this conversation with my teacher. I felt this strange sense of guilt because while my siblings supported me at home, my teacher lending a listening ear helped me process my own feelings. Maybe I didn't understand how my mother processed her own feelings?

"It sounds like you're having a really rough time at home. You should keep writing; you're a great writer." She encouraged me, placing her hand in mine.

"Thanks, Mrs. Webb," I nodded, wiping away my tears.

"I'll tell you what, you can submit this assignment to me today and tonight you have no homework. You deserve a little break."

"Thank you again," I replied to Mrs. Webb, and she gave me a reassuring look.

"Have a great day. I'll see you tomorrow." Mrs. Webb came over to me and gave me a warm hug.

I got up, grabbed my backpack and walker, and walked out of the classroom. I strolled over to the bench near a tree to sit down. I took off my backpack and placed it next to me while I waited for the next class. Finally, the bell rang and I walked off to my other classes, doing my best to get through the day.

Two o'clock finally rolled around as I made my way to my adapted physical education class. The teacher saw me huffing and puffing. She waved me over and we began working on stretches, push-ups, and sit-ups until 2:45 p.m. Finally, the bell rang to signal the end of the day. "Yes!" I shouted gleefully to myself.

I quickly waved good-bye to the teacher, leaned forward to stabilize my backpack, and headed out to the bench to wait for my sister to pick me up.

I thought about my parents, my siblings, and my classmates. I thought about my future and how I planned to go about it. It wasn't always easy being the youngest in the family. It wasn't easy being a daughter with cerebral palsy. More importantly, I wanted to show my family I was capable of paving my own path.

I heard a honk, jerking me out of my deep thoughts. A red Nissan pulled up. It didn't look like Nhu's car. I scrunched up my face in surprise upon realization, heading toward the car. "Mom, I thought you were supposed to be at work," I said as I opened the door to climb in.

"Your sister's staying late at the hospital for her internship today. I'm picking you up," my mother said, looking stressed. "Hurry up, get in, get in!"

"Oh, I thought she was going to pick me up," I said, feeling disappointed.

"I told her I'd pick you up so she has more time to study." I frowned and sulked in the car.

"Okay, sorry Mom. I was kinda mad because Nhu and I had some things we wanted to talk over, and I would prefer the ride home would be just me and her. I didn't expect you to come get me," I admitted.

I knew both my parents worked long hours but on this particular day, my mother happened to have a day off from the dental office. My engineer father was busy coding like always. "What is up with that attitude? How come you can't tell me things?" She retorted back, glaring at me. My mother's biggest peeve was when her children complained or talked back at her. I stayed quiet. "Don't you ever complain when I am picking you up. Do you understand me? Do you know how many orphan kids in third-world countries would wish to have their parents pick them up?"

"Yes, Mom," I mumbled.

I continued sulking and frowning and eventually, my mother leaned over and noticed.

"What's wrong?" she asked as she continued driving home.

I fought back the urge to yell. "You wouldn't understand. It's complicated."

"Oh, Mai. What don't I understand? I am your mother. I raised you."

I was silent on the rest of my ride home, harboring my insecurity inside. The pressure to live up to her expectations took a toll on me. My mother was strict because she wanted me to have a better life than her, but I couldn't help wondering if this was too much helicopter parenting.

It was one issue to uphold my parents' image of an obedient daughter, and it was another to speak up for myself and my needs. I felt like I was standing on a bridge with two life choices between me: follow my own heart or live my parents' dream. When we arrived home, I wasted no time in grabbing my backpack, opening the car door, and coming to the car's trunk to grab my walker and letting myself into the house by punching in the lock code.

The door to our house opened and my mother walked in behind me, nudged me, and said, "Slow down. You're going to trip."

"I'm just going to start my homework upstairs," I said after her as she headed to the side closet to put away her car keys and hang up her purse.

Not wanting to provoke her further, I slowed down on my way to the stairs. I grasped on to the rails and made my way up, feeling the weight of my backpack behind me. As I reached my room, I let out a huge sigh of relief, wriggling off the bag and onto my chair. I folded my walker and put it away in one corner of the room and then I threw myself on my bed. I draped a blanket over half of my body, turned to right side, and stared for a minute at the wall.

On the wall was the crucifix and below the crucifix was a holder carrying a small statue of the Virgin Mary. She had her arms stretched out with her blue cloak hanging. I sat in silence. Could I ask her something? I was afraid. The fear came from my pride. I thought I had everything, but at the moment, I was struggling to hold on to the last bit of faith I had in me. Fear and anger were two emotions that made me lose focus on the goals ahead. I closed my eyes, clasping my hands together and uttered my usual prayer. "Hail Mary, full of grace…"

I sat up after reciting the prayer, pulling the blankets off me, and stood up stretching my arms in the air. I breathed in, paused, and then breathed out. Then I pulled my homework from my bag, pulled out my chair, and sat down. I reached over to the pencil holder, retrieving a mechanical pencil, and began my homework, engrossing myself deeper into the assignments. I understood why some students would say school was one of their escapes from reality. A bunch of thoughts came up for me, rattling my anxiety as a chill ran down my back. I was confused as to how I could find my faith in such a conflict with my mother.

This nagging feeling tugged at my heart whenever I had to make a decision. I cared about what my parents thought. Maybe that was what it felt like to grow up in the best of both worlds. One world depicted respect and consideration, almost like those Lunar New Year occasions when the adults would wish young people well and success in their careers and vice versa. The other world was me trying to find my way, speaking up for myself, and setting healthy boundaries. I sighed once again and put my pencil down this time as I completed my homework, tucking it away in my backpack for the next day.

I headed downstairs, closing the bedroom door behind me. An aromatic smell from the kitchen filled the house. Tonight, my mother cooked phở, one of my favorite dishes. I heard the footsteps of my siblings behind me. "That smells good, Mom!" Hồng-an remarked cheerfully. I, on the other hand, still mulled over the bitter incident earlier in the day. Như and Minh helped themselves in the kitchen, getting some chopsticks and spoons. Liên and Linh pulled the chairs out to get ready for dinner.

My mother paused her stirring of the big pot of broth. "How was school today, kids?"

Before we could answer, the front doorknob began rattling and opened to reveal our father, who was visibly tired from work.

"Sorry, there was a lot of traffic on the way home." My father hung his work briefcase in the front closet and hurriedly kicked off his shoes. "Let's pray and eat." My mother turned off the stove while Như started sorting the noodles for each bowl. Then we sat down at the dinner table, taking up one another's hands to pray, and Linh began the prayer, "Bless this food that we are about to eat, our home, and our family. Amen."

My siblings and father helped themselves to a bowl of phở while my mother sat beside me, handing me the bowl after her turn. I ate in silence, glancing up once in a while to see if anyone noticed. Sure enough, Như asked me, "You seem awfully quiet today, Mai. Are you okay?"

I didn't answer her. Instead, I grabbed my napkin and pulled a pencil from my pocket, scribbling a note to her. I handed it to her and she nodded, acknowledging me. Another hour passed and all the bowls were empty. Chopsticks were laid on top of the bowls with scattered napkins half-dipped in leftover broth. My mother got up first, and then my father and all my siblings gathered the dishes. They stood together and washed the dishes.

After the dishes were put away, Như and I walked upstairs together to my room and sat together sharing our stories about growing up. We cried and batted at our tears. She reached over and hugged me and caressed my hair. "I know Mom can be tough sometimes but she had her own struggles too. Also, you're the strongest person I know. Don't let her words break you, okay? We're all in this journey together."

"Okay, sis. By the way..."

"What, Mai?"

"Thanks for being here. I needed this conversation."

"Of course. You should rest. It's late."

I nodded and helped myself get into bed. Như adjusted my pillow and draped a blanket over me. "Good night." She then got up and turned off the light, closing the door behind her.

CHAPTER 9

POWERLESS

The next morning, I woke up groggily to the sound of my buzzing alarm. I reached over to press the snooze button. "Oh gosh..." In that moment, I stood up and went to the mirror and stared at my reflection. I paced around a bit, confused about the time of day because I had been so stressed about school.

Finally, I glanced at my calendar on the wall and realized it was actually the weekend. I moved to my chair and sat down at my laptop, opening it up to find something on Netflix to watch when I decided to check my email.

I logged into the email and scrolled through it slowly when an unread message caught my eye. The subject line read: *Sunset High School Writing Contest—Please Read.*

I sat up straighter and clicked on it while my heart was beating faster every moment. I opened the email, which had been sent by Mrs. Webb.

> Dear Mai,
> I am pleased to announce that you have been selected to enter Sunset High School's annual Writing Contest. I have nominated your memoir essay because I believe you have great

potential. You should be very proud of yourself. Enclosed in this email, you will find the details to confirm your RSVP and the time to attend. I hope you have a wonderful day and congratulations again!

Mrs. Webb.

I looked at the email again, reading each word carefully and scrolling down further to find the invitation attachment. A rush of excitement went through me and a huge smile spread across my face, basking in this accomplishment. I breathed deeply. Already, I felt a lighter load in my heart. I closed my eyes and prayed for strength but also offered up my gratitude.

A moment later, I opened my eyes when I heard a knock on my bedroom door. "Who's there?" I called out.

"Mai?" My mother's voice seemed to get louder and stronger. "Can I come in?"

I groaned. "Give me a minute, Mom!" I stood up, pacing back and forth.

"Just open the door now. I want to talk to you!" I could sense the urgency in her voice from behind my bedroom door. I put my hand on the doorknob. It turned slightly and then the door opened to my mom looking stressed and slightly annoyed. "Did you finish your homework?"

"Mom, it's Saturday; I have no school."

"Did you study for your SAT yet? How about your grade in math?" My mother pushed her way into my room, moving past me at the door to go and sit on my bed.

"Mom, I'm in ninth grade. I'm not a baby," I said firmly, my voice slightly rising. I went over to my desk, preparing to be scolded.

"I am worried about you. You're not doing too well in math." She crossed her arms and shifted her body in frustration. My mother sighed, putting her arms on her forehead.

"I should be able to decide what to do with my life right? Grades don't define me as a person. It's not the end of the world. Mom, just listen to me. Please."

I wished she'd stop judging me so strongly. Perhaps it was me? Her making decisions for me was out of fear, not love. That fear prevented me from exercising my confidence when I needed to make a decision.

"Teens these days..." she muttered under her breath. I wondered how she must have felt when she was a teenager herself dealing with my grandmother.

"Here, take a look," I grabbed the laptop from my desk and showed it to her.

My mother peered at the email, reading slowly. I could see her face scrunching up in surprise as she turned slightly to look at me and then turn back to look at the screen.

She frowned. "Is this writing contest going to affect your grade?"

"Of course not, Mother! You worry too much, do you know that? You're supposed to be the mother I can talk to, you know? You're supposed to support my dreams, and what do you do? Besides, I just got this email today and I haven't even considered submitting yet." I looked at her with a straight face.

"So, what is this writing contest at school anyway?" my mother asked, her eyes raising in a half-serious-half-disappointed look. My mother probably thought I was a disgrace for being the obvious black sheep in the family. Như studied all the time. Hồng-an and Liên avoided her as much as possible and she didn't care. Minh was a loose cannon and he'd just ignore whatever she said anyway.

"Mrs. Webb, my English teacher, recommended that I enter this contest because I have a strong writing potential." I looked down at my desk, organizing the pile of books neatly to distract myself a little bit.

My mother gave me a look of disapproval. "You should be studying for your SATs. It'll boost your chance to go to college."

I longed to have a healthy conversation with her, but I was nowhere near that point. I longed to understand her like a friend where she and I could converse with ease without us judging each other.

"Mom, I still have three years left to worry about all that. I promise I'll do well if you loosen up and not be so worked up about me," I said, attempting to convince her once more.

"I don't care if it's three years, five years, or whatever! Think about your future!"

"Mom, I don't want to have this conversation. I'm tired." My mother shook her head. "Whatever I do, it isn't enough for you, is it, Mother? Seriously, I just got the email and I haven't even had time to respond to Mrs. Webb's invitation. You just walked in on me. When I had a C on a math quiz in middle school, you were disappointed. A C is passing to some people, but to you that makes me a failure? That's unreasonable." I spoke, feeling my voice break. I turned away from her, avoiding her icy glare.

My mother sat still, shocked at my ability to go against her wishes. I had always been taught not to disrespect or talk back to elders because it's a disgrace. It was so much different than what I was taught in school to speak up and express my opinions. There should be a balance between both worlds, right? I struggled with this so often.

I continued, "What's wrong with being a writer for a career? Or an artist? Or a film director perhaps? In three years, I have to decide on where to go to college and you're just deciding my career based on what you think I should do. Geez, Mom, not everyone is made out to be in a STEM field. At least I should be able to make my own small decisions," I said, standing up now, looking down at her visibly upset face.

It really irked me that she seemed to push her future plans for me when I was still struggling to figure out my own aspirations.

I had done it again; I had pushed her button. It was so hard not to though. She didn't grow up in America. She grew up in Vietnam, a land of rice fields, buffalo, dirt, and candles in place of lamps. She wore tattered clothes when she was little and lived in general poverty. School and her dreams of having a well-paying job were her way out of it. The lack of emotional support from her parents had forced her to rely on herself to look for resources and make something of herself. She didn't have time to sit down and relax.

My siblings and I became the product of immigrant success and in my mother's eyes, it was up to us to continue the legacy of hard work and perseverance she had started. But this meant following her rules and living the life she dictated to us. I struggled with this and couldn't help but feel like my mother had lost out on following her own dreams in order to survive. My poor mom. I did not want to be like that. I wanted to follow my dream.

"What's this?" Mom asked, picking up my journal on my desk. She abruptly opened the journal, landing it on the page where I had written a quote by C.S. Lewis. *"You can make anything by writing."* She looked at me, her eyebrows raising up.

I turned around and looked at her. "Mom, what are you doing?"

"What is this writing?" she asked, her eyes widening as she read every word.

"Mom! No! Please don't!" I touched her arm, trying to stop her from throwing my journal onto the ground.

Too late. The journal landed on the floor.

"You're a disgrace to this family!" she shouted, walking toward my bedroom door. Her long, black hair swayed behind her as she marched away.

"Mom, I can explain!" I moved toward her, trying once more to reason with her.

"I don't need your explanation." My mother stormed out of my room, slamming my door behind her.

I sobbed uncontrollably on my bed for a while after, letting the tears fall without wiping them away. I realized the bad dream I had on the day of my surgery years before had come true. I was struggling to break free of restrictions without damaging my relationship with my mother.

I prayed my mother would come to a better understanding of what I wanted to do in life. However, it wasn't as easy as I thought because she had her own struggles too. I didn't dare ask her what she had gone through before America. I only knew she and my father had survived a war in Vietnam before escaping for a better life like many other refugee families. She would always tell my siblings and I to make education our first priority.

Có học là có tất cả con ơi! When you get an education, you'll have everything!

I knew an education wasn't just about being successful in school. There were many ways to learn besides school; the whole world could be a learning experience. Perhaps, there was more to my mother that I didn't know, but as a teen trying to figure out her own sense of self in this confusing stage of life, I couldn't figure out a proper way to set boundaries with her.

For the rest of the day, I stayed inside my room, not even going downstairs for dinner. The anxiety kept creeping up, and soon the whole day had passed me by. I opened the blinds in my room to quietly watch the last rays of sunlight disappear on the horizon as night settled in. I tried to keep my eyes open but felt them drooping. Finally, I collapsed onto my bed and slipped into a deep sleep.

It was difficult to embrace the pain in my heart, but I was willing to stand up for myself no matter what.

CHAPTER 10

IT TAKES A VILLAGE

Sometime later, I woke up from my slumber to a knock on my bedroom door. I glanced at the clock and realized it was past eight o'clock in the evening.

"It's me, Hồng-an. Can I come in, sis?"

"Go ahead; the door's unlocked."

I got up, pulled the blankets off me, straightened my hair, and glanced at my face in the mirror; my eyes were still swollen and red from crying. The door opened and Hồng-an walked in to see me standing in front of the mirror.

"Are you okay, sis?" Hồng-an asked. She came over and stood behind me with her hand on my shoulders as a supportive gesture.

"I just don't understand how Mom can be so strict with me when I'm the youngest out of all you guys. At least she leaves you all alone." We walked over to my bed and I laid down, laying my head on her lap.

Hồng-an looked down at me, caressing my hair. "She's hard on us as well, so you're not alone. I overheard the fight earlier about the writing contest, I think you should let Mom be. She's a strict mother, but you have all the support from us, your siblings. She'll come around, I promise. Writing is your gift, and it should not be wasted."

"Thanks, sis. I appreciate it. It has been a really long time since we last talked. I am sorry. I am just so focused on school, you know?" I grew quiet after that, reflecting on the conversation.

After a while, I sat up and hugged her. Hồng-an spoke up. "I know school is important, but you have to remember to take care of yourself too, Mai. Self-care and compassion are crucial as well. Healthy body, healthy mind."

"But Hồng-an, what about Mom?" I asked, still locked in her embrace.

"She has her own stress to worry about." Hồng-an continued, running her hand through my hair. "Don't sweat it, sis. You just have to keep moving toward your goal of being a future writer."

"Hồng-an, I'm trying to live my life. We're all trying to live our lives. I just want Mom to loosen up. I know she can be a bit too much sometimes," I said, pausing for a bit before continuing, "Besides, she has no idea what it's like to go through school here. I just feel like every time she pushes her expectations on us, it makes me cringe." I stood up now, grabbing my laptop, and opening it to Mrs. Webb's email.

Before Hồng-an could answer, a second loud knock came on the door. I opened it to the rest of my siblings screaming happily in my face.

"Yoo-hoo, who's the boss lady over here!" they all said in unison. They encircled me and came forward, enveloping me in a group hug. I gasped, taken aback by this sudden acknowledgment and outpouring of sibling love and support.

"I thought you all were busy." My mouth was hanging open, and my eyes lit up at the sight of my siblings' excitement. "How did you all know? I didn't even tell you guys yet!"

"Oh, we overheard the fight from our own rooms. You were so brave to stand up to her," Như said, giving me a half hug. She walked over to my desk and grabbed my journal, proclaiming, "You should document this day. I know it's hard for you to stand up to Mom and speak for yourself. You should be proud of yourself too."

I gave Như a confused look. "Don't get me wrong. I love her, but she's a toughie, Như," I said, finally releasing myself of repressed feelings I had held on to for so long. I wasn't used to this acknowledgment due to the constant criticism and the lack of emotional support from our mother.

"Oh honey, I can feel your pain in your voice. We've all been through what you've been through. Mom expressed her care differently. I mean, she raised six children. You being the youngest and going through medical challenges… That's quite a journey for her. That's not insecurity, that's setting boundaries. I am guessing her protective instincts are a little stronger with you," Như explained.

Minh chimed in, "Here's the thing. If you are going to enter the writing contest, you might as well have a personal board of directors to help you through, am I right?" He flexed his arms to emphasize his point. Strangely today, he smelled really fresh and clean unlike his normal, sweaty look. I wanted to compliment him somehow but held back for fear that he would throw some shady response at me.

"What is up with you today, Minh? Normally, you'd be bouncing a basketball in the yard with your headphones on, ignoring all of us, especially me," I said in surprise.

"You think a guy can't change his ways? Have some faith in me, Mai." Minh stood up and broke into a Michael Jackson moon walk across my room. "Let me tell you who this awesome girl is. She's my amazing sister, Mai!" He pumped his fist in the air and then finished off with a bow.

"I guess... Thanks for the support. It means a lot coming from you. If you can help Mom loosen up, I'd really appreciate it very much." I laughed as I saw him bust out his moves.

"Minh's right, Mai. If at first you don't succeed, try, try again," Linh said.

"Y'all are the best. Thanks, guys. Y'all are the best siblings a sister could have."

"We're always here for you, sis. Every step of the way." Như gave me a pat on the back.

All of my siblings stood up, smiled at me, and then one by one, each of them gave me a high five and left my room.

A new epiphany rose within me after they had all left, and I logged into my laptop again, typing a response to Mrs. Webb.

> Dear Mrs. Webb,
> Thank you for letting me know about the writing contest. I enjoyed drafting this piece and then finalizing it. Please feel free to submit my essay to this contest; I'd like to participate. Thank you so much for believing in me. I hope that I will win something and learn more about my calling to be a writer. You are the best English teacher I have ever met.
> Best,
> Mai

My hands were shaking as I nervously hit the "send" button. Some opportunities happen only once in a lifetime and

I would not miss out on mine. As I waited for Mrs. Webb's response, my phone rang and I picked up the call.

"Hello, this is Mai speaking."

"Mai, it's Tanya! Did you get that email from Mrs. Webb? About the writing contest?"

"Tanya, you got it too? That's means we're both participating!" I shouted excitedly now.

"Yes, yes, yes!" I could hear Tanya's enthusiasm on the other end of line. I jumped into the bed again letting myself laugh without a care in the world.

***

A week went by before I heard anything back from Mrs. Webb about the writing contest.

After everyone had left the classroom once class ended, Tanya and I walked up to Mrs. Webb's desk where she was cleaning up for the day.

"Mrs. Webb, you said earlier in class that you wanted to give us something?" Tanya asked.

"Oh yes. Here's the invitation for tonight's event." Mrs. Webb handed both of us a bright golden invitation. Sprawled across the card were the words *Sunset High School Annual Writing Contest.*

"Wow. Oh my gosh. We did it!" I high fived Tanya, feeling elated, a big grin plastered across my face.

"You both deserve it, girls. I'll see you tonight."

"Thanks, Mrs. Webb."

"You got it."

We walked out of class together, weaving through the crowd of students outside. I wondered if my mother was coming to my writing contest tonight.

"Mai? Yoo-hoo, Mai!" Tanya waved her arms up and down at me, but I was dazed and in another world. I felt the floor shake underneath me. Tanya tried to grab my arm, but it was too late.

Thump. Down I fell.

"Are you okay, Mai?" Tanya's face furrowed with concern. She offered her hands and I grabbed them as she helped me to stand back up. I took a deep breath and dusted myself off. We continued walking through the hallways to the school's office doors. Finally, the noise from the crowd died down, and there was only the two of us.

I leaned over to Tanya and said, "What did you write about?"

"I wrote about the time we met in middle school algebra class. It was also about how I saw you with a walker. Your bravery drew me toward you. You were so worried about your grade in math, and then you opened up to me." Tanya shifted positions and held my other hand to prevent me from falling.

"Oh god. How do you remember all this, girl? I forgot about it a long time ago." I paused, breathed in, and then looked straight ahead as we were nearing the parking lot of the school.

"Gosh girl, we lived those moments together remember?" Tanya let go of my arm this time. "You got it, Mai? Don't trip."

"I won't, girl. I mean, I will fall occasionally, but then I'll get right back up. That's just how my cerebral palsy is. I didn't want to remember, Tanya. It was too traumatizing for me."

"Mai, listen. Sometimes traumatizing moments can turn into beautiful stories."

"That's true." I turned and looked her straight in the eyes.

"I want to write this story because it's our friendship story. That's the power of stories. These words stir people's souls." Tanya and I walked a bit further and then sat down on our usual bench.

"Wow, you're going to make me cry, Tanya. I don't deserve you as a friend."

"Please don't say that. You're in my life for a reason, Mai. You see, I also have some issues of my own. But that's what makes us unique, right?

"Why didn't you tell me all this when we were in middle school?"

"I thought nobody would understand. You see, math was my favorite subject. I was obsessed with numbers. I preferred solving math problems rather than interacting with people. It's difficult for me because I was always in my own little world. You are actually the first person I really opened up to though." Tanya let out a huge sigh of relief, as she finally revealed to me her feelings.

"Really? I didn't realize you were so lonely," I said, patting her arm in support.

"It's just hard for me to open up to people sometimes."

"Oh. Why did it take so long for you to tell me this?" I sighed.

"What do you mean, Mai?"

"Oh, never mind, Tanya."

"What is it? Don't you dare keep secrets from me. I always tell you everything."

"No, I don't think I can tell you this. It might hurt your feelings." I stopped myself, feeling a pink blush on my face.

"Mai, you and I have been friends since middle school. What's going on?" Tanya frowned.

"No, there's nothing wrong. I just never realized you and I are so similar. We both have a hard time fitting in."

"Oh, yeah, but that doesn't mean we can't make it in the world. We just have to celebrate ourselves," Tanya said, moving her long hair out of her face.

"It's hard for me to be vulnerable too. My parents didn't really encourage me to talk about my feelings, so they were repressed. I feel trapped. Stuck. Depressed." I broke down. The tears came. For a moment, I turned away from Tanya.

"It's okay. You don't have to explain it if you don't want to. We're still best friends and that will not change."

"Hey, I'm gonna go to class Tanya. I'll see you afterward."

Tanya nodded and we parted ways to go to our respective classes. The day went by quickly as I walked to each class, sat down, and participated unwillingly.

The bell finally buzzed at 2:45 p.m., just as I finished my exercises for PE class. As I headed out of class, Tanya stood waiting for me.

"How was PE class, bud?"

"Not too bad. Thanks for listening earlier this morning. It's just that my mom's a hard person to understand, I guess… I'll see you tonight?"

"Yes, see you tonight, Mai. It's our big day. Hopefully, we'll win something."

"I'm praying for it to go well. Let's do this!" I sat in reflective silence with her until I saw my ride pull up. Như and Linh were already waiting for me in the car near the gate of our school.

"Hey! I'm over here!" I yelled to her car. Như pulled up to the curb. She turned to her side door and pressed a button to unlock the door and let me in. Tanya and I parted ways as she walked off a separate path to wait for her mother.

"How was school today?" Như asked as I reached over to put my seat belt on.

"School was great! Guess what tonight is?"

"What, Mai?"

"Today is finally the day the school will announce the winners of the writing contest." I gestured with my hands in the air excitedly.

"What time will the event be at, Mai?" Như said as she put the keys in the ignition.

"It's at seven o'clock tonight, Như. Can you can try to get Mom and Dad to come? I know all of you will come, but I am not too sure about them."

"I am pretty sure Dad will come. I'm so proud of you, Mai." Như turned to me and smiled.

"I am proud of you too, Mai," Linh said.

"Thanks, guys."

Như drove both of us home with a proud smile on her face. I thought about the love my siblings had given me when I felt down or depressed. When times were hard, siblings were gifts who could never be replaced. It was a great reminder that a huge support system was crucial for my well-being.

CHAPTER 11

AN OPPORTUNITY

As soon as we got home, Như followed behind me halfway into the house to make sure I didn't fall and then went to her room once she knew I was okay on my own. I walked upstairs to my room, put my backpack down, and pulled out my English binder. I pulled out the golden invitation from inside the binder and looked it over once again happily, tracing the fancy letters on the RSVP card. Tonight would be my big night.

A smile spread across my face as I realized my writing's impact. As I was thinking about this, I glanced at the clock in my room and realized it was almost 4:00 p.m. I had about three hours to prepare for the event tonight. Quickly, I ran to Linh's room and knocked on the door.

"Come in," Linh said from behind her bedroom door. I turned the doorknob and entered into Linh's bedroom, hopping onto her bed. "Congratulations, sis. We'll see you tonight at school."

"Can you help me do my makeup before tonight?"

Linh nodded at my request. "Sure thing, sis. Anything for you. I am so proud of you!"

I blushed a little. "Thanks."

I walked downstairs afterward to grab a small meal to eat. As I moved toward the dining room table, I saw there was already a bowl of rice along with spam meat, cucumbers, and soup with a note next to it.

> *I am working late tonight. Heat up your food and enjoy. Don't forget to finish your homework.*
> —Mom

Instantly, I felt a chill run through me. I was overcome with guilt when it hit me that this was my mother's way of expressing her love and care for me. She may not have fared well with open communication and heart-to heart conversations, but she definitely showed it through her cooking. I sat and ate my food while reflecting on this gesture.

After I ate, I walked back upstairs to my room to get some homework done.

I forgot for a moment that I was anxious. As long as my father and siblings came, that was all that mattered.

***

Later that evening, Như drove me and the rest of my family to school. As soon as she parked the car, I opened the door and ran inside. I slowed down a bit to prevent myself from tripping over.

"Tanya!" I called, waving at a crowd of students and parents. I spotted her wearing a casual, flower print dress and sitting by herself near the stage. I headed over and sat next to her.

The theater was adorned with gold banners and white covers on the chairs. Conversations filled with joy and excitement rang out among parents and students throughout the theater, and there was light music playing in the background.

I leaned forward to give Tanya a hug. At that moment, Như, Linh, Minh, Liên, Hồng-an, and my father caught up with me and they all shook Tanya's hand. I felt the happy tears welling up in my eyes. My dad had been a strict man. He wanted a better life for me and my siblings. Today was the first time I saw my father interact with my best friend, and my siblings were happy I was following my passion.

"Hi, my name is Mr. Tran. I'm Mai's dad."

"Nice to meet you, Mr. Tran. I'm Tanya and I've been friends with Mai since middle school. Let's all go inside. I can't wait to hear who wins the writing contest.

"Where are your parents?" my father asked Tanya.

"Oh, my mom will be here a little later."

I nudged Tanya on the shoulder. I whispered: "Did you tell her the event is tonight?"

Tanya cupped her hands and whispered back, "She has to go to work and she'll be late."

We sat, conversing in low voices while waiting for the ceremony to start. I was so nervous at this point and could barely believe this was all happening. It was the first step toward my dream and I could feel the adrenaline rushing through me. I must have been showing signs of my nervousness because Tanya smiled at me and reached out to squeeze my hand for comfort.

"You look nervous, Mai. Relax. It's our most important night." Tanya put her hand on my back as a gesture of support. She looked so beautiful.

I smiled at Tanya, knowing with her by my side, I could get through anything.

"It's incredibly difficult, but what keeps me going is our friendship and what you taught me over the years. Was it difficult for you to make friends before you met me?" I wondered, my eyes widening.

"Oh, yeah, definitely. I was shy, and someone actually told me to go make friends. Do you know what they said to me?"

"What?" I asked, hiding my shock. This was another side to Tanya I didn't know.

"They told me to go make friends and my response was, 'I'm my own best friend.' I think I had a point there. If you don't love yourself first, how can you love others? True change must begin with ourselves. That's why you're such an inspiration to me, Mai." Tanya paused to fix her hair.

"Me? An inspiration? Are you kidding, Tanya? That's just who I am, girl," I responded.

"You're an inspiration, Mai. A true example of what it means to persevere in the face of hardships."

"Again, that's just who I am, Tanya. Everyone can be an inspiration, but that's just how I am. I don't think I should be viewed as an inspiration just because I have cerebral palsy. I just want to be me."

"I also owe your friendship to making me realize that if you could make it through with your cerebral palsy and succeed academically, all while trying to slowly foster your family relationships, then you deserve credit for always standing strong. I should learn a lot more from you." She glanced over at the clock on the wall to check the time.

"You're too kind. Thank you so much Tanya. I learned from you too."

Soon enough, Mrs. Webb walked across the stage, stepping up to the podium and speaking into the microphone. She looked beautiful as ever in a long, navy blue dress.

"Hello families, friends, and students, it is my honor to welcome you all to the annual writing competition at Sunset High School. I would like to announce that we have two students this year who made it to the final round. Please join me in congratulating Mai Tran and Tanya Johnson. They are scholars and examples of what it means to persevere through trials and tribulations. Both Mai and Tanya are well-deserving of this award. Mai herself has had to overcome her disability to get here. Tanya worked hard as well. I am honored to say these two students are the two winners of tonight's competition."

Tanya and I linked arms and walked up to the stage. We extended our arms out and Mrs. Webb handed us our awards and cash. My ears were deafened by the sound of loud applause. I turned around and saw my father and siblings standing up and clapping for me. The whole row of seats had parents of my classmates in a standing ovation. It was then I realized for the first time in my life that I had stood up to my insecurity and fear. I had done it. Tonight, I purposely did not bring my walker because I wanted to prove to myself I could walk without relying on it too much.

I stood on stage with Tanya for a little while, and I saw there were local reporters from the community showing up. I heard the endless clicks and was blinded by the flashes of the cameras. One reporter, donned with her mic and dressed in a formal professional suit, asked me what my future plans were.

"You're a great writer. Is this what you plan to do in the future?" She flashed a genuine smile and waited. I froze for a minute and turned to Tanya, feeling my knees shaking. I reached out to grab Tanya's hand to stabilize my balance. I had never stood on stage for this long or had been asked such an important question.

Tanya leaned over and whispered in my ear, "It's okay. Just be yourself. Remember, people will know that's the real you when you speak your truth. Go on, Mai. Tell her."

I took a deep breath and responded, "It has always been a dream of mine to write and tell my story. I owed this accomplishment to my family, especially my siblings, my parents, my physical therapists, and my best friend who is here right next to me. To me, I can have all the accomplishments in the world. Who knows what will be next for me in the future. What's most important to me here and now is following my heart and knowing how to tune in with my mental well-being." I stopped, breathed, and realized these words affirmed the beginning of self-acceptance and confidence in me.

The audience had a moment of silence. I looked out to the sea of faces and spotted Tanya's mother coming into the door in a hurry. She sat down and waved at both of us. I nudged at Tanya and pointed. "Look, there's your mom."

Tanya nodded and sighed, feeling a wave of calm over her as she saw her mother made it just in time before it was her turn to answer.

"Thank you for sharing such insightful words, Mai." The reporter smiled once again and bent down to scribble notes of my response. Then she moved on to Tanya and asked the same question.

Tanya looked straight into the camera and confidently said, "Of course. Thank you for the question. I met my friend Mai in math class in middle school. Math is my favorite subject, but I also loved writing too. I know it's important for me to have friends like Mai because people like her can teach us a lot about love, acceptance, and strength in the face of trials. She has taught me that the connections we have with people around us are important because it's necessary for our mental and emotional well-being." She paused for a moment and thanked the reporter.

The reporter took notes once again. "Thank you so much for answering the questions."

Tanya blushed at me. "Gosh, I am so flattered. You didn't have to be that extra."

Before I could answer, I felt a hand on my shoulder and turned around to see Mrs. Webb.

"You both may go back to your seats. Those were really great answers. I am so proud of you!" Mrs. Webb said with a smile.

I gripped Tanya's hand for balance and we walked backstage while the camera still flashed behind us. The loud applause of parents and students nearly deafened our ears.

Finally, the intermission time came and we sat down next to each other in a corner and had a moment to ourselves.

"See, Mai? That wasn't so bad. You actually stepped out of your comfort zone and did it!" I am so proud of you. Err, I mean of us!" Tanya high fived me and we walked down the steps from the backstage back to our seats.

After the intermission, Tanya sat next to her mother in the same row as my family. Our faces were still giddy from the all-star moment earlier.

"Hi, Mom! I am glad you made it just in time to hear me answer the reporter's question. Are you enjoying the program so far?" Mrs. Johnson turned, nodded proudly, and hugged Tanya.

I glanced over at them, feeling a pang of guilt. *If only my mother could make it. I wished she'd understand.* I pushed that thought away and turned to my family on the other side of the same row.

"You did it! We're so proud of you!" My siblings said in unison. I looked at them, their smiles showing the pride and happiness.

"That's my daughter!" My father beamed proudly. He grabbed me and enveloped me in a tight embrace, temporarily cutting off my air supply for a second.

"Whoa, *Ba*. Let me breathe." He loosened his grip and I sat up straight, watching the rest of the program for the evening, cheering and clapping for other students who participated.

At 10:00 p.m., Mrs. Webb finally came on stage and gave her last remarks, congratulating us both once again as well as acknowledging the honorary student pieces that were submitted. The curtains came down and the lights turned on.

Tanya's mom and my family hugged us once again, chatting among themselves. I knew this writing contest was a small sign of progress toward healing. We headed out the door afterward in the cool night. Tanya said goodbye to me and headed home with her mother.

I continued walking slowly to the parking lot with my family. Halfway there, I stopped and looked up the night sky with the bright moon staring down at me.

"Look *Ba*, isn't the moon pretty today?" I asked my father.

"Yes, *con*. Yes, my daughter. *Các anh chị và ba rất tự hào về con. Ba nghỉ Má củng vậy luôn!* Your siblings and I are very proud of you. I think Mom is, too!"

I nodded and smiled. We finally got to our car and drove home.

CHAPTER 12

BOUNDARIES AND SPIRITUAL COMFORT

After that eventful night of the contest, I came to a revelation about my writing abilities. I was no longer that insecure freshman, and I gained a new understanding of boundaries and making choices for myself, even if those choices brought disapproval from my mother. Before long, sophomore year came and went. Not much happened during that year, other than the fact that I dealt with the sudden death of my paternal grandmother who had long been suffering from dementia.

Then junior year came and now I was overcome with new expectations in my academics: studying for the dreaded SAT tests and deciding on colleges.

The Saturday morning sun peeked in through the window as I lay on my bed, thinking of all the future endeavors I had yet to complete. I flipped over onto my stomach, holding my journal and reading through each word I had written so far. Some entries were sad and others were just the roller-coaster of emotions that I experienced while I was dealing with teenage angst.

I had come a long way, but sometimes still doubted myself. I questioned myself and my ability to surpass the boundaries set by my family and my culture, but mainly, my mother. I leaned over and grabbed my phone to dial Tanya. Three rings later, she picked up, her cheerful voice ringing on the other end.

"Hello?"

"Hey, Tanya!" I replied, my tone less cheerful than hers.

"Hey, Mai, what's up? You sound a little bummed out? Everything okay?"

"Well, yeah, I guess. I mean, I was just thinking about that writing competition we participated in back in freshman year and I was remembering the moment we both walked across the stage after winning and how everyone cheered for us; I felt so special that day. It was one of the happiest days of my life."

"You're brave," Tanya said, like she always did. As long as I had my best friend Tanya by my side, nothing could deter my goals of being a writer. We talked and laughed about our lives, the crazy world of parental pressures, the similarities of us navigating through life with disabilities and ableism. We talked for hours and before long, I glanced at the clock and realized it was almost two o'clock in the afternoon.

"Hey, friend, I gotta go. Thanks for listening."

"Anytime, Mai! Bye!" I heard the telltale clicking sound of Tanya hanging up the phone on her end.

I always felt better after talking to Tanya because it truly felt like she was always on my side whenever I had issues or insecurities. Although I had my siblings, Tanya was a good friend and someone other than my family who I could talk to. She encouraged me to speak my mind, which was the opposite of what was taught in my house. In my house, speaking up for one's own opinion was a sign of disrespect, and listening to my elders and parents meant I was meeting the obligations of a respectful and meek daughter. Perhaps, it wasn't the speaking up that I was the most concerned about, but the way I went about communicating with my parents across our cultural barriers.

I was obviously raised in an American culture while trying to balance my Vietnamese culture and hold on to its traditions. Right now, I was struggling with both, like standing on a balance beam and trying hard not to fall off. Maybe I could compromise and take a bit of both.

I closed my phone and lay back down, about to close my eyes when I heard a knock on my bedroom door. I had heard that knock so many times before. I groaned, getting myself off the bed. Just like that, all the confidence in me was buried as I walked to the door, opened it slightly, and saw my mother standing there on the other side.

"Who were you talking to?" my mother interrogated, pushing my door open wider and stepping inside. She placed her hands on her hips, a suspicious look on her face as she stared hard at me. Her shirt smelled of onion and soy sauce, which made me wonder how she had even heard my conversation with Tanya if she'd been in the kitchen cooking.

"No one," I mumbled, half holding back the urge to yell.

"Stop crying! Why are you crying? I only asked you a question and you're getting all teary like a baby!" my mother said as she hovered over me.

"You wouldn't understand," I said, my voice cracking. I felt like Jerry the mouse escaping from Tom the cat, only I didn't have the means to come back with an appropriate excuse. "Um..." I tried again, feeling the emotional rocket ship within me shaking and about to burst.

"What?"

"Never mind, Mom..." I began, letting the words trail off.

I suddenly wanted to ask her why she didn't take time off to attend my writing contest freshman year, even though I knew she had been busy working. I wanted to know her better, but every conversation turned into a big misunderstanding. I attempted to open up to her, only to get berated for my feelings or choices. She always seemed to judge me based on my decisions.

I heard footsteps coming up the stairs and my father appeared in the doorway of my room, intervening to stop our argument. He moved to stand next to my mother.

"Khánh, calm down. You can tell her in a firm voice," my father said, holding on to my mother's shoulders.

"Hung, stay out of this. Let me have a conversation with her," my mother said sternly.

Finally, I could not control my emotions any longer and shouted, "Who decided what's my future? You think you're some kind of god?" I felt all the anger rush out from me. It felt ridiculously great to finally let this little traumatized voice yell out the repressed emotions I had held in for so long.

My mother stopped and looked at me in shock. She tried to speak but I said loudly in Vietnamese, *"Không, con không muốn nói chuyện với Má. Má cho con được yên tĩnh!"* No, I don't want to talk to you right now. Please leave me alone.

"Mai, use a gentle voice with your mom or you're grounded for a week," my father reprimanded me. In a proper world, I preferred his consistent voice telling me what to do rather than me having to hear my mother demand things of me.

Then both of my parents turned to leave, moving into their own bedroom and praying for me. I heard the strong but firm prayers droning on and on. "Hail Mary, full of grace!..." My father had called my siblings in as I listened to the prayers in the next room.

They continued to pray the rosary fifty-two more times while I sat, letting my tears come tumbling out in a big puddle on my tired, overwhelmed face. I was done being forced to follow my mother's expectations of being a pharmacist.

How could I have a better relationship with my mother when all I could see was the toxic emotions I felt every time I interacted with her? Did I have a choice? It seemed like I didn't. I wished my mother was more westernized, but of course, that wouldn't be possible. She was a traditional Vietnamese mother from head to toe.

I laid down on my bed and draped a blanket over me, turning over to stare at the wall. I tried to think positively, telling myself I was a good writer, that I could follow my dreams. But that little voice of doubt grew stronger, telling me I was worthless, I shouldn't have been born, and no one would love me with my cerebral palsy.

As I battled with those thoughts, I found comfort in prayer and in silence. In the silence, I felt this warm, spiritual embrace washing away all my pain. When no one listened to me, there was a higher being, a god, that I could call on whenever I needed Him. Maybe at this moment, God was trying tell me something.

It finally dawned on me that this was what silence meant. I came to the realization that silence meant slowing down and finding God in all things. After a while, I sat up and reached over to grab a tissue on my desk, wiping away my tears.

I took out my journal to write.

> *Dear Lord,*
> *I am feeling so overwhelmed at the moment. The stress of living up to my parents' expectations is a burden too great to bear. Please help me. It is hard*

to follow my own dreams. What can I do? I want to write and be the voice for the voiceless. I want to be strong and I want to make my parents proud of me. Maybe I can do both? Lord, please help me be a better person. I am scared of what my parents would think. Please, Lord.

Amen

I finished dumping my heartache, closed the journal, and took a nap, falling into a lovely dream.

In my dream, I was walking in a field of flowers without a care in the world. Roses, daisies, and tulips covered me as I ran laughing. Only in my dreams did I feel understood. It was a world where I got to imagine my ability to rise above my hardships.

Suddenly, I saw my grandma coming toward me down a beautiful, golden staircase decorated in flowers. She was dressed in a long, white, angelic dress and behind her, the sky was illuminated with bright clouds and a group of angels followed her down. A mist of warm air surrounded me, and I felt the weightless sensation overtake my body.

"Mai! How are you, my sweet granddaughter?" She enveloped me in a tight embrace and planted a doting kiss on my head.

"Grandma! Oh, how I miss you." My heart swelled up with happiness as I felt this feeling of spiritual elevation rising toward my chest.

"I miss you, too, sweet baby. I have been watching you from heaven. Can you feel my presence?" she asked, still locking me in her hug.

"I feel you in my prayers every night, Grandma," I proclaimed eagerly.

"Oh, my dear granddaughter. How are your parents?"

"My dad has gotten better. He supports me. My mom? She's still a little hard on me."

"Don't be so sad, my dear. Your mom just worries about you a lot more."

"I know that, Grandma. It's just hard because of Mom."

"Oh honey, you have a long way to go. But don't worry, I'm watching over you from heaven."

"Yes, Grandma."

"Write more, my dear. Your words are power. Use it well and don't let anything stop you from your dreams. Remember who you are and where you came from."

"Thanks, Grandma."

"Promise me you'll never lose your passion for writing." Her face shone like a bright sun in the sky as she gave me that peaceful smile of hers.

"I got it, Grandma. I promise."

"That's my sweet granddaughter. I believe in you." She caressed me once more before letting go and disappearing from sight.

I jolted awake from my nap.

Grandma knew what was going on and she was watching over me. A slight smile spread across my face. Silently, I clasped my hands together in gratitude and sat still. All the memories came floating back to me. She talked on and on about the old tales of her ancestors and how she and my grandpa married each other. Even though I didn't understand what it meant at the time, my grandma was passing down these stories unknowingly in the hopes that someone would write them down.

I sat up and took out my other journal. I scribbled down the words my grandma had told me in my dreams. *Stories matter. If I don't write them down, then who will?* I clenched my fist and silently promised myself I would never let that fire of determination die out within me.

As I comforted myself and confronted my feelings about my mother, I couldn't help but realize that like any mother, her concern for my future stemmed out of her own upbringing. I didn't yet dare to ask her why she felt the way she did though, for fear those questions would bring up her traumatized past.

As I continued to scribble down the words of my inner turmoil, I felt a small voice from within me urging me to keep going. I wanted to know what experiences my mother lived through, but I couldn't bring myself to ask her about them.

The repressed emotions, like bad weeds in the winter, kept gnawing at my self-esteem. I wanted my mother to understand me, and I wanted to understand her. I could only hope one day we would.

CHAPTER 13

A MOTHER'S PAIN

A few days later, my mother came into my room and sat across from me on my bed. Her face was stoic, her demeanor reserved.

"I can't believe you would do this to us. All those years of raising you and taking care of you and your siblings..." she began. Her expression shifted and I could see on her face how visibly tired she was, with baggy eyes and dark circles from lack of sleep.

"Mom, I did nothing wrong," I stated, reaching out and holding on to her arms. *Please Lord. Please. Help me talk to her.* I prayed, turning away momentarily to collect myself mentally.

"You have such a rebellious streak!" my mother snapped, standing up. She sighed again, throwing her arms up in frustration. She was so desperate to maintain control over me that she hadn't realized I was growing up.

"Geez, Mom, I'm only sixteen! Why are you putting so much pressure on me?" My eyes glared at her as I protested. I got up from my bed and walked over to my desk, pulling out my journal and ripping out a few blank pages, half to prove my point and half to relieve myself of the anger I felt inside of me.

"Mai, life has more to offer you. Why don't you go for a STEM career? It's possible." She paused, biting her lips. "You're still so young, and you have your whole life ahead of you…" The most annoying thing was when she gave me life advice before hearing my side of the story.

"I despise you, Mom!" I shouted, unable to hold it in any longer. I sighed, feeling my body shaking as my face shifted. I thought of my mother having a strong aversion to me asking for any ounce of empathy and understanding of my situation. I tried to push away the bitter voice inside of me, but it somehow won that battle and I whimpered softly as I raised my hand to bat at the tears before they fell on the floor.

My mother bent forward slightly and looked me straight in the eye, her hands grasping both of my shoulders. "Just be grateful. You don't know how much it takes to raise all six of you, and all I want for you is to do well in school so you won't have it hard in life." I couldn't understand why my mother placed so much emphasis on school when she hadn't realized I'd been trying so hard to do what she wanted while maintaining my needs and growing irritation at exercising my independence.

"Ugh, why do you keep thinking I am so ungrateful to you? I don't understand you at all!" I said in frustration.

"Do you know what's it's like to be poor? To hear bombs constantly near your window and to be afraid of war? No, you don't. I saw those tragedies every day and thought how when my children are here, I would do everything I can for you all to have a successful future. *Sướng mà không biết hưởng!* You're privileged and you don't even know it!"

"But Mom, you and I are from different generations. We are in different times now so you're *not* helping me by discouraging me from what I am good at," I begged almost to the breaking point. I then waved my mother away, pointing her toward the door. "You can't dictate my career choices. Please let me have some space; I have my own life to live and my own decisions to make." I paused, taking a deep breath to keep myself from lashing out again.

Mom didn't say anything after that. She just stared at me for a minute before turning and leaving my room.

When the door clicked shut behind her, I laid down on my bed, turned over, and sobbed into my pillow, realizing maybe I should have said something calmer to my mother. I felt empty and hollow inside because of the failed attempts at communication.

Although I still had Như, the rest of my siblings, and my father, I was figuring out the maze of my life and decisions. I felt like an ant stuck in the dirt and trying to crawl its way through back to the colony.

A little while later, I took out my phone to call Tanya. The phone rang three times before she picked up on the fourth ring.

"Hello?" I said, hopeful that Tanya would pick up the cues that I wasn't having a great day.

"Hi, bestie, what's up?" I burst into tears. Tanya remained quiet on the other end for a few minutes until my crying had calmed a bit, then she asked, "What's wrong? Is it your mom again?"

I paused for a moment. "Yes..."

"Mai, have you ever asked about your mom's story? Or maybe let her open up to you?" Tanya asked carefully. I could feel that she didn't want to tread on my emotions given the timing and the fragility of the situation.

"It's hard to get my mom to listen to what I have to say. Just send me good vibes and hope this situation passes."

"Of course. You're going to be okay. Just let it go. I am sure your mom will come around," she said eagerly.

I twisted my hair in my fingers nervously, feeling the anxiety coming on. "Tanya, please don't turn into my mother! She always gives me one of those life talks!" I smiled a little.

"Aww, Mai, you're a real trooper." Tanya said, giving a small laugh on the other end of the phone.

"Thank you." I laughed back. "Oh gosh. you're making me laugh so hard."

"That's what I want to hear from you. The laughter. The cheer. The usual sunshine."

"Aww, thank you." I sat up, feeling a bit better.

"Let me know if you need anything, but for now I gotta go, Mai. Bye!"

"Okay..." We both hung up.

I sat down at my desk after the call, reaching out to trace the fading colors of my desk while I thought. My mind wandered and the old feelings of despair came back even though I had spoken to Tanya.

All my life I'd been the youngest, the disabled, and the helpless. Mom was always strict on me. That was the one issue I couldn't understand. She may have come here as an immigrant with my father, raving about the opportunities she gave me and my siblings, but she could not grasp that there were many ways to succeed in life.

I went back to my bed again, flopping onto the bedspread. For a moment, reality came back to me as I pondered a plan to hold myself up. I wondered about my life, the memories of my childhood coming back to me. The years of my siblings helping me exercise, the time I took my first real steps with my therapist Anne, and even the times my mother picked me up when I had fallen. Now that I turned sixteen years old, she expected more from me because she wanted to relish in bragging about us, her children, as trophy children. Or perhaps this was her way of developing a thick skin in us?

Rather than instilling confidence in my following my own passion as a writer, my mother did the opposite and stepped on my self-esteem, bringing me down. The American Dream for my parents wasn't easy, but I also had my own issues and ideas of the path I wanted to take in life. At this point in time, my emotions were like a roller coaster and I needed my own space.

Doing well in school was one thing and finding my career was another. Balancing the two priorities in addition to living with cerebral palsy was a mountain I still had to climb. A lump formed in my throat as I felt the weight of life upon me. It was the feeling of sinking, of not being good enough, and not being worthy enough.

Then there was the issue about pleasing my parents while keeping my inner, critical voice quiet. The more I pushed that voice back, the stronger it got. I wanted to have those deep talks and walks with my mother but first, I had to figure out her story and what she experienced. There were many layers I wanted to uncover within me and, as her daughter, I longed to find my way back. But each time I reached out, the door to my understanding and willingness to try snapped shut. I was blind to placing boundaries and controlling my emotions.

My parents had sacrificed so much and I knew I wanted to do better by them, but being better seemed to mean being forced to be someone I was not. I closed my eyes again, reflecting in silence and trying to navigate this confusing stage of my teenage years. Could I come out of this storm with more resilience? I pondered about letting go and getting help because I felt like I was on a rocky boat, and that boat was slowly sinking under the winds and storms of life.

Perseverance, I reminded myself silently. Through it all, there was still light somewhere in the dark; I just had to find it somehow.

CHAPTER 14

PANIC ATTACK

―

The time passed by quickly and soon it was seven o'clock in the evening. I dragged myself downstairs to dinner, walking slowly to avoid tripping over. I was still stressed from overthinking my relationship with my mother and had somehow mustered up the courage to sit at the dinner table. All I wanted to do was carry my food back to my room. If I was by myself, there was no chance of me getting into an argument.

But my mother scolded me when I arrived. "Sit down, you're late to the table and that's an inconvenience to everyone waiting for you!" All my siblings were already there at the table, but they didn't dare say anything. One of my mother's other pet peeves was anyone trying to comment on her opinion when she was talking directly to me. I secretly wished my siblings would calm my mother down, but I knew it was better if they told her in private. I bit my lip and kept a straight face.

"I was taking care of some stuff, Mom," I reasoned, while pulling out a chair to sit down.

"What were you doing upstairs, Mai?" my mother asked, heading to the cupboard to grab some chopsticks.

"Mom? I thought you wanted me to study hard. That's why I stayed up there."

"Well, you need to manage your time better if that's the case." She sat down next to my father and reminded him to say grace. Once he had, we began eating.

My mother had this specific perception about time. She didn't want anyone in my family to waste any minute relaxing. She wanted us to focus on academics and our future even if it was years away. I had a hard time accepting this and preferred to spend my time otherwise, though I also knew I had to get through high school and graduate.

My father spoke up. "Khánh, let her eat first. Then you can talk about managing time with her. Mai, you can go ahead and eat. I'll talk to Mom later," he said, gesturing to keep the peace. I nodded, sitting quietly and focusing on eating my dinner. I fought the urge to go back to my room. Mom stayed quiet and didn't say anything else.

"You okay, sis?" Như asked, passing me a bowl. "Here, eat some rice." She scooped some rice into my bowl. "Pass me the salad, Hồng-an," Như said, extending her arms out.

Hồng-an passed Như the salad and she was about to scoop some salad into my bowl when I refused and waved it away.

"No, Như, I'm good. Thanks for helping me with the food." I fidgeted once again, holding the spoon as I tasted the rice. The food was strangely bland and dry. I tried to swallow and take another bite, but my taste buds seemed to develop an aversion.

After dinner, I helped my family with the dishes and wiped down the table. I planned on talking to my parents about getting therapy but decided against it. Perhaps I could talk to my siblings, but they seemed busy with their own needs. I walked back upstairs to my bedroom.

I laid down again, feeling tears rise up and fall down my face.

From downstairs, I heard Mom and Dad closing the front door behind them, shouting to us, "We're going out to a movie. The dishes are done, but please clean up after yourselves and vacuum the floors!"

"Okay, let's clean up, and head to bed soon. Where's Mai? Hồng-an, can you go check on her?" I could hear Như ask.

I laid there on my bed, huffing and puffing, becoming aware that it was becoming harder and harder to breathe. Nonstop thoughts were running through my mind, and I had a flashback of the conversation with my mother and how terrified I had felt of disappointment and shame. A sharp pain shot though my chest and I didn't know if my heart was going to stop beating or if it was just me imagining things. I shut my eyes and then opened them again, but all I could see was a blur. I reached over to my face but suddenly pulled my hand back. I tried to sit up but was exhausted. My chest felt so heavy now.

I heard Hồng-an's footsteps heading up the stairs and then she opened my door to see me, laying there, shaking. The chills shot up my body and my head felt hot and tingly. Then I started sweating profusely, unable to stop shaking.

"Hồng-an!" I jerked out of fear.

"Mai, calm down, it's me. You're in a daze. She stared at my bulging eyes and saw me hyperventilating.

She called down the stairs to my other siblings, "Y'all! Mai's breathing is too fast!" My siblings heard and came up to see what all the commotion was about.

"No, no, no, Hồng-an," I groaned.

"No, I am right here. It's okay." Hồng-an pulled me into a hug, not letting me go. She rubbed my back and made sure I was stabilized.

"Mai, are you okay?" Như asked me. I was too exhausted to answer her. "Minh, go grab me a face cloth. Everyone, calm down. Mai's going to be okay. Linh and Liên, can you both make sure there are no heavy objects near where she is?"

They both nodded and stood up, scanning the surroundings. They saw a lamp cord near where I was and wrapped it up, moving it to the corner of my room to the floor near my desk.

Hồng-an grabbed her phone from her pocket, dialing 911. "Hi, yes, I am calling for my sister. She's breathing fast and sweating."

I laid there on my bed listening as Hồng-an explained the circumstances of the situation and my current condition and listened to the instructions of what to do before she hung up the phone. My other siblings stayed by my side and watched me.

"Okay, we're taking you to urgent care. C'mon, let's go," Hồng-an stated.

I nodded and covered my face. I felt ashamed but knew I needed help. My siblings helped me up and together we walked downstairs, where Hồng-an grabbed the car keys and we headed out.

When we got to the van, Hồng-an helped me into the front passenger seat and then went to get into the driver's seat. My other siblings piled into the back, and we all made the sign of the cross on our foreheads before Hồng-an started the car and backed out of the driveway. On the way, Hồng-an glanced at me at every stoplight to make sure my condition wasn't getting any worse.

Ten minutes later, we arrived at the hospital where the staff checked us in. We sat down and waited a while before a medical assistant called my name and led us into the exam room.

"I'm Trisha," she said, checking my vital signs. She asked me some questions about my medical history next, and when she was done, she made her way to the door. "The attending doctor will be with you in a bit," she said.

While we waited for the doctor, I mustered all the strength I had and said to my siblings, "Please don't tell Mom and Dad. They will freak out," I begged, pleading with my eyes. I just knew Mom would freak out if she knew and would probably tell me to "pray it away" instead of getting actual help for what I knew was a mental health issue. It occurred to me in that moment that mental health and getting help overall was an uncommon thing in the Asian culture.

"We won't tell them," my siblings all reassured me, heads nodding in mutual agreement.

"Thank you," I whispered, relief washing through me.

Hồng-an placed her hand in mine. "Sweetie, all I want is for you to be safe and healthy. Also, I've seen how you handle your cerebral palsy condition while going through school, and how you've also had to deal with a lot of pressure from Mom." All my other siblings encircled me, each placing a hand on my shoulders in acknowledgment.

I thought about the events leading up to my panic attack and a wave of guilt washed over me. I knew this moment was hard to process, but I also knew I would be on my way toward my recovery journey.

"Mai? Are you there?" Hồng-an waved her arms at my face. "Come back to earth, sis. You're in a daze."

"Huh?" I asked, finally paying attention to my sister who was hovering over me.

"You're in a daze. Are you okay?"

I nodded and stayed silent, gripping tightly onto my sister's hand. My face and forehead felt hot and shaky. Somehow, amid all the trauma I had experienced, a small voice inside me reminded me there was a way. I fought off the nagging sensation of uncertainty and held on to that strength.

Finally, the attending doctor stepped into the room and greeted me and my siblings, shaking their hands first and then mine. He reached over to retrieve the pen on the side of his ear with one hand while holding on to the clipboard full of papers in the other. He pulled a chair from the corner of the room and sat down.

He looked over my chart while Hồng-an continued to hold my hand for reassurance. The doctor turned to me and moved his stereoscope from his neck to his ear and placed it on four corners of my chest. He listened for a while, glanced at my chart, and said, "So I see here that Mai has cerebral palsy and a history of seizures? It's important to not overdo activities when she has these conditions. It looks like, based on her symptoms, she had a mild panic attack. I will give her a small dose of Benadryl to help her relax."

"Yes, she's been pretty stressed lately with home life and trying to keep up in school," Hồng-an responded calmly. My other siblings stood there, listening and nodding.

The doctor looked at us with kind eyes and compassion. "Sounds like you are going through a lot. In the meantime, I recommend you look into getting therapy to help with the stress."

"Thank you, Doctor," my siblings said in unison. The doctor stepped out of the room to give us some alone time. My siblings leaned over toward me and I reminded them again quietly to keep the situation from our parents.

Hồng-an nodded and said, "We promise. Do you want anything to eat? One of us could get you a sandwich or juice." I perked up a little.

"Sure, just don't leave me."

"Oh, honey. We'll never leave you," Hồng-an reassured me.

I breathed in deeply again but could still feel the fear within me trying to release.

"The rest of us will be here with you while Hồng-an goes to grab food for you," Như said.

"I'll be right back." Hồng-an stepped out of the room leaving me with my other siblings, who gathered around for comfort. Hồng-an came back a few minutes later with a sandwich and juice, passing over the juice while she fiddled with the sandwich wrapper. "Here is your food, sis," Hồng-an said as she peeled off the wrapper and handed me the sandwich.

"Thanks." I bit into my sandwich ready to eat, but just like dinner, it tasted bland and dry. A pang of hunger rose in me and despite my efforts to feel better, I was sinking in despair.

"Hồng-an?" I looked up at her.

"Hmm?" She reached over and brushed some loose hair off of my forehead. I took a deep breath. "I know my life is meaningful, but I'm not myself lately and it's going to take more than praying to get over this."

Hồng-an nodded, acknowledging my distress.

"Yes, you will be okay," Như chimed in, giving me a reassuring smile.

"I was stressed and then it led to all this mess," I confessed, feeling the tears falling from my eyes again.

Linh grasped my hand and said, "Hey, you got this!" Liên flashed me a smile and gave me a thumbs up while Minh held out his headphones, gesturing to me to listen to music.

I shook my head, but appreciated his kind offer.

Hồng-an made eye contact with me and grasped both of my hands. "Listen, Mai. Don't let Mom's words get to you. Real talk. It's gonna hurt more if you keep dwelling on it. There'll be more bumps in life, and I know it's tough, but you got me and our siblings." I nodded and held on to her hands. Then we linked pinkies and I felt a wave of relief washing over me.

"I guess you're right. I'll try not to dwell on this whole career talk anymore; it annoys the heck out of me to keep telling Mom," I shivered.

Hồng-an rubbed my hands together for warmth. "I hear you." Hồng-an's cell phone rang and she picked it up right away.

"Hello, Hồng-an speaking." She stood up and stepped out of the exam room as I looked on, worried if it was Mom suddenly calling because she somehow knew what had happened to me. I felt my anxiety rising again. A few minutes later, Hồng-an walked back in.

Hồng-an had tears in her eyes. This was the first time I had seen her cry. She had always been strong. The sister I could rely on. My older sister who was always there for me whenever I needed her. She was the sister who thought of everyone and tried her best to be the peacemaker of the family.

In my culture, I saw many young people like me who had succumbed to their parents' unrealistic expectations and fallen into a vicious cycle of insecurity. But this was the first time I had ever seen my sister being so vulnerable and unafraid to show her emotions.

"Why are you crying?" Guilt washed over me as I looked at my sister's stressed face.

"Oh, it's all right. I just worry about you."

"Hồng-an, did something happen? Are you okay?" I looked at my sister with concern.

"I'm fine, baby. Don't worry. I just want you to know you are loved." My sister reached over to the side table and plucked a tissue from the box there, wiping her tears away.

"I'm alive, aren't I? I am right in front of you; I will be okay."

"Are you really okay, baby? You looked so stressed out. That's not the Mai I know." She pressed her lips together, keeping a straight face now.

"What do you mean? Hồng-an, who were you on the phone with earlier?" I could feel my lips heading downward.

Hồng-an took a deep breath. "Mom, and Dad were wondering where we were."

"Oh? Mom and Dad didn't find out about my panic attack, did they?" I asked, my eyes widened with every word that came out of my mouth. Mom would question everything I went through and that would spell disaster and break her trust with me.

"No. I told them we were out for the evening spending time together," Hồng-an admitted to me. I started crying again.

"Do you want to go home now?" Linh asked, plucking a tissue off the box on the table and wiping away my tears for me.

"Yes, guys. I'm really tired." A queasy feeling overtook my body and rose to my throat. I placed my hand over my chest.

"Oh no, oh no, Mai," Hồng-an grabbed a trashcan and placed it near my mouth just in time for me to throw up into it. Như and Minh rushed out to the vending machine to grab me some water. I hated throwing up, and I hated being at the hospital. Everyone always had to take care of me, and I hated that too.

"Do you want me to call the nurse? They might have something to settle your stomach?" Hồng-an suggested.

"No, I just want you here. Don't leave me."

Hồng-an squeezed my hand and put her head down on my hospital bed to collect herself before lifting it up and making eye contact with me. She managed a tiny smile, but I could feel that her heart was breaking inside for me.

"Hồng-an, I'm scared of what Mom will think." I managed to stop my tears but felt comfortable that I was finally acknowledging my internal wound.

"Mai, honey, rest. You've had a long day today." I could hear the pain and the urgency in Hồng-an's voice while fighting the growing negative voice in my own mind. I clenched my teeth and quietly counted until I had calmed down.

"That's right, Mai. You've had a long day," Như reminded me gently.

I looked the other way and asked in a quieter voice, "Hồng-an?"

"Hmm?" She caressed my hair softly.

"Tomorrow is Sunday. Monday is school. I'm gonna fall behind for sure. Summer is coming soon." I felt my body shaking again. *Breathe.* I reminded myself.

"I know. You have your last year of high school looming over you. But don't worry too much about that. You'll be fine," Linh encouraged me cautiously.

All my other siblings helped me gather my things to get ready for check-out. Hồng-an walked out to find the doctor so she could sign the hospital papers, and the rest of my siblings helped me off of the exam table. A small voice in me arose again and as I looked around at how understanding and helpful my siblings were being, I realized for the first time that getting help for my mental health was not something I should be ashamed of.

CHAPTER 15

SURVIVAL MODE

―

The doctor came back into my room with Hồng-an not long after she had left to find him.

"You are good to be discharged, Mai. Make sure to take care of yourself, have someone check in with you, and just take time to rest and relax, all right?"

"Yes, Doctor." I nodded.

"Also, I'm going to refer you to a therapist. Her name is Luann Glason. She can also speak Vietnamese if your parents need more information about the importance of mental health." He handed Hồng-an a Post-it Note scribbled with Luann's contact information.

"Thanks again, Doctor. I appreciate all your help." I shook his hand firmly.

"You're very welcome, Mai. Take care of yourself." He turned and left.

Hồng-an and the rest of my siblings walked out after him. I held on to Hồng-an's arms to keep myself from falling. Once we made it to the parking lot, Hồng-an stopped, put the Post-it Note away in her purse, and took out her keys.

"Y'all wait here. I'll go get the car," Hồng-an said, walking out into the parking lot.

While my other siblings and I waited for Hồng-an to drive around, Liên and Như stepped up to put their arms around me in a loose hug.

"You survived, sis," Như said with a soft smile.

"This shall pass and you'll come out of the darkness to shine at full brightness because that's who you are," Liên added. Minh and Linh each came up and gave me a hug too. I nodded my head, grateful for their care. I hadn't been this close to my siblings in a long time.

"Thanks for being here. I appreciate all of you putting up with me." I felt myself finally starting to relax.

Hồng-an pulled up a moment later and we all got into the van. On the way home, I reflected on the whole ordeal I had just been through and realized happiness would come from practicing self-care regardless of my circumstances. That was where I had been struggling up until now and knew I needed to start putting myself first for the sake of my mental health.

***

When we arrived home late in the evening, my siblings helped walk me in, observing me to make sure I was okay. When we got to the front door, Như punched in the code and we all made our way into the house, only to find it quiet and dark. My siblings and I were about to get up the stairs when we decided to wander into the kitchen and found a plate of apple pie with ice cream for us. There was a note accompanying the dessert:

> *Enjoy your dessert. We're heading to bed. It's late.*
> *Wash those dishes when you are done.*
> *Love Ba and Má*

I looked at my siblings with my mouth hanging open. This was one of the few times my parents left us alone. Usually, I was accustomed to my parents being overbearing. I managed a tiny smile and high fived each of my siblings mouthing, "No parents!"

We headed to the bathroom to wash our hands and then sat down to eat our dessert. Twenty minutes later, we were full. I stood up and helped clean and put bowls away, going back and forth between the dining table and the sink.

My siblings walked ahead of me and stood there, turning on the faucet and running their fingers through the water to test the heat level. I stood next to them and lowered myself into one of the bottom cabinets, about to grab some fresh gloves, when they all turned to me and stopped me.

"You've had a long night. Why don't you go upstairs and rest? We'll take care of the dishes."

"Thanks." I went to the dining table where Hồng-an had left her purse. "Can I open your purse and get my therapy referral note?" I called out to her, turning to see her poke her head out from the kitchen.

"Go ahead," she nodded. I quickly unzipped her purse to retrieve the note.

Normally, I would have been questioning my worth after something like this, wondering if I had done enough for the family and worrying about my mother and what she thought of me. Instead, this time, the doctor's advice came to my mind and I was reminded to take care of myself. I nodded silently as I pulled out the note, calling out, "I'm heading to bed now."

I turned to head up the stairs, putting my hands on the rails to keep my balance as I heard Linh reminding me from the kitchen, "Be careful and watch your step. We don't want you to trip."

"I'm okay, I got this. Don't worry," I said as I continued to make my way up toward my room. Once I was in and had shut the door behind me, I immediately took out my journal and wrote questions to God instead of the usual heartache dump.

> *Dear God,*
> *God, are you still there? Can you hear me? I am sorry I wasn't thinking clearly. I feel anxious about all of this. What is my purpose? Is my calling to write? I want to develop a real bond with you, Lord. The kind where I could talk to you about everything and anything. My senior year is coming soon. What will you have in store for me? I still feel like I have to live up my mother's expectations too. What do you both want for me? Just give me a sign. Anything will do, Lord. I promise I will go to Mass more often than just Sundays, you know? Lord, please tell me what to do.*
> *Amen*

I closed my journal and climbed into bed. As I closed my eyes, I began whispering the Memorare prayer. Eventually, I slipped into a deep slumber.

***

The next morning, I woke up and peeled the blankets off of my body before standing up to fold them and head downstairs. I took my time walking when I heard voices talking quietly in the dining room, but finally, I reached the last step of the stairs and saw my parents were awake.

My mother sat at the table, visibly stressed but quiet. She kept a straight, serious face and gestured for me to sit down. I calmly pulled out a chair and waited for her to start scolding me when instead, she reached over and touched my face. I looked ahead and saw my father near the water dispenser, filling two mugs before coming back to sit next to my mother.

They both sat quietly for a bit before my mom asked, "Are you okay? We heard what happened from Như, but we're glad you were safe with your siblings."

"Um…" I hesitated now, deliberating whether or not I should tell my parents the whole story or not. I put my head down, and said in a small voice, "Please ask my siblings to come down." Before my parents could even call them, I heard their footsteps already making their way down the stairs.

In just a few moments, my siblings had all gathered at the table around me, some sitting and others standing near me for support.

"Mom, Dad, we want to talk to you," Như said.

My father spoke up, "We are concerned for you, Mai, especially your mother." I stayed silent.

Hồng-an filled them in on the news, "Mai's having a rough time with balancing school and home life right now," she began, glancing at me to make sure I was okay with her telling them. I nodded my head slightly and she pressed on. "I was with her last night at the hospital and the doctor said she needs to find a balance that works for her. He recommended she should go to therapy for help with this."

My parents sat quietly, taking in everything Hồng-an was saying. It was hard for me to tell how they were taking the news as their faces didn't give anything away.

"She's been wanting to tell you both about needing help for a while, but didn't know how to go about it," Như added from beside me, her hand reaching out to cover mine in a show of open support. I nodded in agreement with her statement, feeling my anxiety starting to creep up again as I waited for my parents' response.

My father looked at my mother and nudged her. "Well?" She sighed and I could sense her growing irritation coming.

"Why do you need therapy? Don't you know you have everything?" She turned away from me then.

"Mom, she's going through a lot," Hồng-an replied, pleading with our mother to be understanding.

"Please hear her out," Liên pipped up.

I began to cry silently, both moved by my siblings show of support in front of my parents and saddened by my mother's lack of empathy. My mother frowned harder at the sight of my tears, shaking her head.

"Ay, ay, ay. Stop crying," she chastised me. I looked over at Hồng-an sadly.

"See, Mom didn't understand what you were trying to say either." It was straight up proof that when it came to me, she refused to listen or see reason.

"All right, all right, that's enough for today. I think your mother needs some time to process this," my father finally said, putting an end to the conversation. My mother abruptly stood up from the table then and, doing her best not to look at me, headed upstairs, my father right behind her.

That left the rest of us sitting and standing around the dining table and wondering what had gone wrong to make this an unsuccessful dialogue.

"It's okay. Just dust yourself off and pick your strength back up," Như said.

Minh grabbed a tissue from the box near the water dispenser and handed it to me.

"Thanks, bro. I needed this time together. I just wish it didn't have to happen this way. I am sorry I always judged you for being the loose cannon of our family, but I think you're the most carefree sibling out of all of us."

Minh shrugged. "No biggie. Don't sweat it, sis. It's just a part of growing up."

I leaned on to Hồng-an to stabilize my balance while Linh and Liên stood there, both reminding me to breathe.

"Inhale. Hold for ten seconds. Okay, exhale. You can do this, sis," Linh encouraged me.

I took multiple breaths in and out, holding them for ten seconds each as Linh instructed. I did this until I felt my shoulders finally relax and the anxiety ease.

"Thanks, y'all. I'm better now," I murmured.

My siblings smiled at me and that's when I realized that in spite of what I'd been through, my failed attempts at communication with my mother, the pressures of school weighting on me, and the trauma of dealing with my disability, God had given me the gift of siblings. A priceless group of biological friends who had seen my ups and downs and still stood by me and helped lift me up unconditionally.

Then they all walked with me to the living room and made sure I was safe before going back to their rooms. I knelt on my knees on the carpet with my head slightly bowed and uttered a prayer of gratitude. *This will take time.*

CHAPTER 16

IT TAKES COURAGE TO FACE THE TRUTH

―

Later that same evening, after I had gone back to my room for some quiet time, I heard a knock at my door. I got up from my bed, where I had been sprawled out writing in my journal, and walked to my bedroom door.

"Who's there?"

"Mai? It's me, Ba," my father called through the door. I turned the knob and found him leaning on the door frame looking exhausted from work with his wrinkled work clothes and frazzled hair. He let himself in and moved to sit at my desk, watching me quietly as I went back to plop down on my bed. I expected him to bring up the conflict with my mother from early this morning, but he surprised me.

Instead, he calmly asked, "What's going on, honey? You seem not quite yourself lately."

I sighed.

"Dad, can I tell you something?" I could feel my anxiety rising, though it did not feel as bad as when I had to talk to my mother. I felt more at ease talking to my father than I ever felt talking to my mother. "I need to be completely honest with you and I need you to hear me out," I said, pushing away the voice of insecurity rising within me.

"I hear you." He rested his chin in his hand and made eye contact with me. I stared at him for a moment, assessing if he was serious before I took a deep breath and finally told him the truth.

"Being a pharmacist is not what I want for my life." The words rushed out of me like a dam breaking open. "I don't see myself doing that after I graduate from college. I am a writer, Ba. I know I am, and that is what I want to do with my life, and what I want to study in college." There was a weird sense of relief that filled me after I had said it, like admitting my feelings to my father was a sort of catharsis, despite the fact that I still felt anxious about his response.

My father sat quietly for a bit, taking in what I had said before smiling softly at me and reaching out to take my hand in his, his thumb gently brushing against my knuckles.

"Thank you for telling me and being honest about your goals," he said. A tiny feeling of excitement arose in me as I realized this knot in my life was slowly untying. My father had not gotten upset, nor was he judging me. Instead, he had acknowledged my feelings and heard what I needed to say. "I hear you, honey," he continued, "I know I might not always seem supportive. Your mother needs me to be on her side too, but remember that day I snuck into your room and found your journal? Or the day you won the writing award at your school? I was so proud of you, and I knew deep down I would support you no matter what."

I nodded, remembering that day. "I am sorry I reacted strongly the way I did because I wasn't sure what you were trying to do, Ba."

My father paused, soaking in my apology and said, "I'm sorry we didn't give you the space you needed to grow. Then, I saw your writing, the poems, your style, and I realized you have a gift. I was overwhelmed with guilt, honey. I realized we, your mother and I, we were expecting too much out of you."

I could feel my eyes beginning to well with tears, though for the first time it was out of happiness as I listened to my father accept me for who I wanted to be.

"Is this real?" I joked lightly, earning a chuckle from my father. "I know you and Mom love me. But sometimes, sometimes—" I stopped, unable to go on as my emotions overwhelmed me. My father leaned over and patted my knee.

"No, it's us. It's not you. Parents should model encouragement for their kids."

"I never thought I'd be hearing this from you." I laughed a little bit looking up at my father. It was the first time I saw my father at his most vulnerable. He had always been the quiet, firm type because in our culture, men were taught to suppress their emotions. In that moment though, I saw my father as a strong man with a soft spot underneath.

"I know. I'm learning about you and your siblings as you grow up here in a world very different from what I grew up in, and I am trying to let go of old traditions that don't fit anymore. Progress is always better." He chuckled, his eyes twinkling now.

"Yeah. Thanks, Dad. I would also appreciate it if you and Mom could give me some space for a bit." My father nodded and we hugged each other for a long time. The warmth of his embrace was new territory for me, but I was excited to explore it moving forward. He let go and we sat side by side in silence. It was a reflective silence that slowly made its way to my heart.

It was then I realized this feeling of silence was a much-needed cursor toward healing for me. I wasn't used to affection, but this was the time I saw my father genuinely making an effort to know me.

I realized that although my parents grew up in a different generation than my siblings and I, navigating this multicultural barrier had taught me more about my own resilience and acceptance. Getting through my changing moods was like being on a roller-coaster ride. I began to understand that rather than focusing on the negativity of the situation, I had to find little things I could be grateful for, like how my siblings helped me, or when my father sat and listened to me talk. That's what finding God in all things meant.

I felt like a butterfly, once a caterpillar, now making its way out of the cocoon on a branch. Could I fly and let go of my insecurity? Only time would tell.

***

My desire to develop a better relationship with my mother was motivated by the success of the conversation I'd had with my father. However, I quickly discovered this goal was not going to be easy.

A few days after the breakthrough with my father, my mother came into my room and attempted to help me make my bed like she usually did. When I put my hand on her arm to stop her, she wasn't exactly happy. It was like the idea of me being independent upset her.

"Mom, I can make my own bed." She frowned at me for a moment before finally moving to sit down at my desk and watch me, as if to make sure I could actually do the task by myself.

"I'm still worried about you," she said bluntly, crossing her arms. "And I know you don't feel like talking to me." She sounded a bit hurt as she said it.

I finished tucking in the sides of my top sheet, trying to think of how to reply to her comment. Finally I took a deep breath and turned to her.

"Mom, I know we butt heads every time we talk," I started, keeping my voice level and calm. "I get frustrated because no matter how much I try, you refuse to listen to what I want. You always say the only way to be successful in life is to major in a STEM-related field." She opened her mouth to cut me off, but I pushed on, not allowing her to interrupt my thoughts. "I know that's what you want for me, but the more I dwell on it, the more it just doesn't sit right with me. STEM might be for some people, like Như, but it's not for me." I felt tears threatening to fill my eyes, but I fought them back. I wanted to appear strong in this moment.

I had finally told my mother, in no uncertain terms, I did not want to pursue a STEM career. This was big progress for me, and I waited anxiously for my mother's reaction, feeling hopeful that she might listen like my father had.

At first she seemed taken aback, then irritated. That gave way to concern and then suddenly I saw tears filling her eyes. I had never seen my mother cry. It caused a wave of sudden guilt and confusion to wash over me as I watched tears trickle down her wrinkled cheeks. I wanted to reach out and embrace her with all my strength, but I resisted, mainly because I couldn't help but think of how often she had hurt me or made me cry, and for a moment I was glad she was the one hurt for once.

Then the guilt started overwhelming me.

"Má, *con xin lỗi. Con xin lỗi.* Mom, I'm sorry. I'm sorry." I began to apologize profusely as a way to try and ease the guilt that was overtaking me. I stepped forward to try and embrace her, but she covered her face in shame and held up her hand to wave me away. I thought about leaving my room to give her some space but instead decided to stay. I stepped forward again and refused to let her turn me away, hugging her tightly.

Was this what it felt like to forgive? I wasn't sure.

I held her for a while as we cried together. It was both strange and cathartic, and it was greatly needed by both of us. Once we had both begun to calm down, I loosened my grip on her and grabbed us both a Kleenex, my mother and I wiping our tears away together.

"Mom, are you all right?" I asked softly. She didn't say a word but kept shaking her head. I tried again. "Will you be all right?" When she still didn't reply, I sighed. "All right, maybe you should go now. I think we both need some space. I hope you'll be okay, Mom."

She nodded and stood up, quickly heading out of my room. I heard her shuffle down the hall to her own room and shut herself in. In her absence, I sat quietly and thought hard about our encounter. It was the first time things hadn't escalated into a fight, and I felt like my mom was also struggling with something she had not shared. I wasn't sure if I was ready to ask her about her story yet, nor was I ready to completely open up to her about all of my hopes and aspirations for the future, but today we had made some progress, even if it had only been to cry together.

I thought about the ongoing struggles we had and knew I was much closer to my siblings than both of my parents. An uneasy feeling crept over me. I could see the hurt and the pain in my mother's eyes when she had sat here crying. It felt like we were strangers from different worlds. Her world consisted of escaping the hard life of a poverty-stricken country and giving opportunities to her children. My world was reaping the benefits of westernized culture and trying to follow my aspirations. Could I reconcile these two worlds and meet her somewhere in the middle?

After a while, I realized it was too dark in my room for the middle of the day. I made my way to the window and threw open my curtains. The sun shone bright in the late afternoon, pouring warm light into my room. I basked in the warmth of it for a bit, feeling it fill my soul, and I felt peace in that moment. I then walked over to my shelf and took out my writing journal. Sitting back down at my desk, I flipped through the pages and reflected on the poems and words I had filled it with.

I reminded myself I still had a long way to go before I could fully recover from the trauma I had suffered through my life.

I made the decision that I wanted to share my journal with my mom, hoping to show her proof of what I had accomplished and what my passion for writing meant to me. I left my room carrying my journal. I first checked her room, but found she wasn't there, so I made my way downstairs. I found her sitting at the dining room table alone.

"Mom?" I called out, walking toward her. I stepped up next to her and was about to hand her my journal, but she refused and waved me away as she had done earlier. The silent dismissal hurt and I shrank back from her, feeling my walls building back up as I tried to protect myself from the emotional pain. I retreated back upstairs in defeat, wanting desperately to talk to someone who did accept me. I went from room to room knocking, but no one seemed to be there. Finally I knocked on Minh's door and it swung open to reveal him standing on the other side looking confused.

"What is it?" he asked.

"Minh? Where are the others? Can you come downstairs to see what's going on with Mom?"

My brother shrugged and said, "She's probably in one of her moods again."

"Oh," I said, feeling even more disappointed that I couldn't get through to her.

"Just give her some time." Minh reassured me. "Have you contacted a therapist yet?"

I shook my head. "No, I feel nervous. It's just too much, and I don't think Mom would approve." Minh nodded his understanding. "Where are the others?" I asked again.

"Our siblings?" They went out to run some errands," he replied. "Listen, Mai. You don't need anyone's approval to get therapy. It's as simple as going to the doctor for a check-up." He informed me, trying to be reassuring. I smiled in response and nodded my head. I liked how my brother kept it real for me even though he was annoying sometimes. Perhaps he was right. Perhaps I needed to take the first step by myself, with or without my mother.

CHAPTER 17

SPIRITUAL MENTORING

───

Sunday rolled around and there was a knock at my bedroom door early in the morning.

"Who's there?" I called out.

"It's Linh, Liên, and Hồng-an. Do you want to go to Mass with us today?" Linh asked me eagerly.

"Sure, let me get ready really quick," I replied through the door. I got up and changed into my Sunday best. I picked my favorite blue flowered dress and walked over to the mirror to look over my reflection. *I am wonderfully made in the image of the Lord. Nothing is going to stop me now.* I smiled at my reflection. I did one last check of my outfit, smoothing down my dress, before I turned to leave my room.

"Ready to go!" I said, opening the door to my three sisters waiting.

"Oh, you look so beautiful, all grown up and dressed up. Just like a princess," Hồng-an said, offering her hand. I smiled and took her hand in mine as we walked down the stairs together and out the door to the car.

We got to the church just in time for the homily. My siblings and I walked in and took our seats in the front row pew. A priest was there in a long, green robe with a picture of Jesus on it. His animated voice boomed over the microphone as he spoke.

"Jesus doesn't tell his disciples they will have to manage without friends. Finding a kindred spirit in the world is always a gift. Tell a friend today: I'm glad we're in this together!" The priest's words moved my heart. As I sat there in the pews listening to him, flashbacks of the first meeting with Tanya in math class came back to me. She was my kindred spirit. God knew I needed her in my life when my world felt lonely. Tanya was a blessing in disguise.

I sat quietly with my siblings and listened to the homily until it was over. After everyone left, except for my siblings and me, I walked to the altar, knelt down, and prayed for a few minutes. My siblings did the same, each of us giving silent thanks to the Lord.

As we finished praying, a voice called out, "Friends, do you need help getting somewhere?" I turned to see the priest facing my siblings and me. He was dressed in clerics this time, and he had a warm smile with a twinkle in his eye.

Hồng-an shook his hand. "Oh, we're just here for my sister today. We decided to go to Mass to help her regain her purpose."

"Oh, is that so? You all are welcome here. I'm Father Josef. It's a pleasure to meet you all." One by one, he shook my siblings' hands and then mine. "What's your name?"

"I'm Mai. I'm almost a senior in high school. This is the first time I've been to Mass in a long time," I sighed, feeling guilty for the confession.

"Oh, that's all right. God knows your broken heart. He wants to come to you in the right time when you are ready. You can find Him in all things and everywhere you go." He reached over to a nearby pew and pulled out a bible, opening it to a specific verse. "Here, this verse is for you." He read to me, "'You can do all things in Christ who strengthens you.'" He looked up and smiled at me. "Whenever you need to talk to God, come find me so I can help you."

"Could I talk to you for a bit today, Father?" I asked, my eyes pleading with anticipation. I shook a little inside. I had just met him, but I already had something I needed to get off my chest. I breathed deeply once again.

Father Josef looked at me with kind eyes and led me over to a pew in the back of the church while my sisters followed behind us. My sisters moved to one corner of the pews and looked on while I conversed with the priest.

"Tell me what's going on in your spiritual life." He sat down next to me, holding on to the bible, ready to open to a passage.

"Well, I've been having a difficult time with my mom. I feel like she's always agitated with me for some reason, and I cannot figure out how God can console me in that. I feel lost, Father. Like, I've always known my faith is here somewhere, but at the moment, it's hard for me." I put my hand over my chest to emphasize my point.

"Ah, I see. That definitely is tough to go through. Have you tried asking how she feels?"

"Well, you know, Father, I am going through the stress of school and figuring out my life. When I become overwhelmed with indecision in whether or not I should follow my love of writing or listen to my parents and go into the healthcare profession, I feel anxious and scared." I leaned back slightly.

Father Josef paused and closed his eyes. He clasped his hands together and prayed to himself. A moment later, he opened his eyes and said, "What is God calling you to do?"

He grasped both of his hands together over his clerics to emphasize a point.

I paused in silence and looked up at the cross on the altar while the priest waited patiently. Tears welled up in my eyes and I batted them away. "I believe I am meant to be a writer. I feel that by writing, I can express myself, heal my own heart, and help others too."

Father Josef made eye contact with me and kindly whispered, "You are not alone. God will walk with you throughout. To Him, you are already precious in His Image. He loves you and He knows what you have been through, so just trust in the process, Mai. He's there." Father Josef pointed to the cross near the altar again. "You see, life will always throw you curve balls. You just have to roll with it, my friend." He paused again, waiting for me.

I burst out with a small laugh. "I always thought God had a serious demeanor all the time. It gets boring at times to have my mother remind me to pray."

"Well, come to think of it, God does have a sense of humor if you talk to him about it. He's in the little moments in the day, the encounters that you go through, the friendships that you have, your family, and small accomplishments like you coming to Mass today. That's a small step toward finding your faith again." Father Josef paused to let me gather my thoughts. His eyes seemed to twinkle brighter than before.

"Father, how did you know you wanted to go into this ministry of serving people?" I asked out of curiosity. I genuinely wanted to know because the priest was so loving and kind. I felt I could open up to him.

"Well, I had a life writing plays before I came to the realization that I wanted to do more. I knew I wanted to help accompany people, like you, through their faith journey and help by meeting them where they are and guiding them through as needed; that's what brings me peace." Father Josef smiled.

"Wow, you were a writer too?" My eyes lit up in delight. I was feeling very glad I had gone to church; God definitely knew what I needed.

"Indeed, Mai. It's important to follow your heart. As for your mother, she is still learning and coming to terms with you maturing, I'm sure." Father Josef looked up at the cross again and asked, "What do you think God would do in this situation?"

I paused, putting my hands under my chin, deep in thought. "Well, He would understand and forgive, right Father?"

"You know it. It is okay if you are not there yet because you are still thinking things through and God is waiting with you. Just give your mother space, pray, discern, and then come to her when you are ready." Father Josef placed his hand over me to give me a blessing.

"Thank you. I better let you get back to your work, Father." We walked back to where my siblings sat waiting.

"You can have her back," Father Josef said, chuckling. His clerics were now wrinkled a bit, but he didn't seem to mind. "I kept her long enough, but we had a great talk. Thank you for coming here today. I am glad I could help. Mai, come see me any time, okay? God bless you all."

"Thank you, Father." My siblings and I stood up one by one, and we shook the priest's hand before making our way back to the car.

As I walked back with my siblings, a new feeling of deeper awareness arose in me as I felt confident in moving past my struggles.

CHAPTER 18

THE EPIPHANY

As we got into the car, Hồng-an put the keys in the ignition and we drove off to our house.

"Father Josef is a nice priest, huh, Mai?

"Yeah, he's so friendly, Hồng-an. Maybe I should ask him to be my spiritual director the next time we come to Mass; what do you all think?" I perked up excitedly at the thought of having one since I had never ventured out of my comfort zone. Asking for help was still a new concept for me. Often in my culture, asking for help was seen as a sign of weakness. But all the interactions I'd had so far were easing me into being vulnerable and seeking help.

"I think he already offered to be your spiritual director, Mai. I saw how he opened up the bible verse that you needed to see and how he invited you to come talk to him when you need help finding God." Hồng-an smiled at me, giving a reassuring pat on my back.

"Do you think I could maybe let go of this feeling of insecurity? You know, I'm still kinda new to accepting and letting go," I questioned, glancing over at her.

"What would you want to let go of?" Liên chimed in, listening intently.

"I don't know. Feelings of not being good enough and not doing enough for the family."

"Yeah, maybe it's something you should talk to the therapist about," Linh suggested, gesturing her hands to indicate her support.

"Yeah, but—" I hesitated, biting my lips.

"But what, Mai?" Hồng-an asked again. She reached over to the glove box to get tissues. "Here, take your time." She handed me a tissue as we stopped at a light.

"Mental health is a hugely sensitive topic. I don't think anyone in our community talks about it much because it is a taboo topic," I said, taking the tissue from her, and dabbing it at my eyes.

"Yeah, I agree, but that's why you have to go to a therapist to help you through these feelings. Stress tires your brain out, and your emotions can go nowhere if they are unresolved," Hồng-an continued while my other two sisters nodded in agreement.

"You sound like a therapist, sis," I observed. I had always looked up to my siblings for these little moments of wisdom. Hồng-an let out a laugh at my comment, glancing over at me.

"I am nowhere near that level of expertise, so don't take my word for it," she replied, returning her gaze to the road.

"Thanks, sis. You're the best!" I may not have been born in the best circumstances, but I had everything I needed in this life. It meant more to me than anything else in the world. Hồng-an smiled as she continued driving.

After we arrived home and as I walked back to my room, I overheard my parents talking to each other from their room. I stopped just outside my door to listen to them talk about giving me space and boundaries. I listened for a little while longer, rather pleased to know they were discussing such a topic, before I went into my room and closed my door. I immediately took out my SAT prep book to prepare for the upcoming test in the spring. Like all students, I hoped to obtain a high score to get into a great school. In this moment, I realized that whatever my score would be, it would not define my worth, my ability to succeed in school, and, more importantly, it would not define my life.

I flipped a page of the book, scribbling some notes in the vocabulary section and then marked my choices. As I worked on the prep book, there were moments when I could feel stress and anxiety creeping up so I exhaled and inhaled a few times, counting for ten seconds with each breath.

After some time, I looked up and made eye contact with the Virgin Mary statue on my shelf, quickly praying to her to help me get a great score on my SATs and thanking her for showing me the light even in the darkness.

She only stared back at me in silence with her gentle eyes, arms out and inviting me to contemplate the silence as my friend.

***

A little while later, I closed the SAT book and walked over to Linh's room. I knocked gently on her door. "Linh?"

"Come in," my sister said from her door. I turned the doorknob and opened it to see her bent over her desk in the corner drawing a picture, her art supplies spread out around her on the desk. She scrunched her eyes, deep in focus.

I stepped into the room, moving to sit on her bed as I watched her working. "Do you have a minute to talk?" I asked her. Linh stopped what she was doing and put her paintbrush down. She reached over to her wipe box and plucked a napkin, wiping her hands off and turning to face me.

"What's up?" she asked.

"I'm okay, Linh. I just want to talk." I paused, breathed deeply, and then started speaking. "So I finally decided to get therapy."

"Good, I am proud of you. You're making progress, Mai. How's school?" she asked eagerly. It had been a long time since I had talked like this to Linh. We lived in the same house and came from same parents, yet I didn't talk to her much due to her quiet nature. She always faded into the background. She loved art of all kinds and would draw every opportunity she got.

"You really are proud of me?" I wondered. It was a bit of a surprise to hear her say it. I knew my siblings had always been there for me, but this was the first time I had heard Linh acknowledging me.

Linh nodded, leaning over to hug me with one arm. She flipped her hair with the other arm as we quietly reflected. "I am sorry I haven't been there for you as much as Như and Hồng-an."

"It's fine. I've been busy too. It has been really hard since I am still trying to figure out what to do with my life." I let go of her now, making eye contact with her.

Linh placed her hands in mine. "I understand. It's hard. But getting therapy is a big step toward healing and recovery," she replied sweetly.

I nodded, scooting close to her and then leaning on her shoulders. We sat in silence together as I braced myself for more questions, but Linh allowed me to simply sit with her quietly. A strange sensation overwhelmed me. Perhaps, for the first time in my life, I didn't feel so held back.

"Linh, how do you feel about our parents? I mean Mom in particular?" I breathed again, trying not to sound awkward. I fiddled with my fingers nervously, keeping my gaze down to avoid eye contact with her; I was nervous about what she would say.

Linh thought for a moment, searching for the right words. "Mom has gone through a lot in her life," she finally said. "And I know she needs time to process that you're growing up. I went through the same experience with her, and I can tell you that you need to create boundaries with her. Give her some space but remember to take care of yourself too." She paused to smile at me. "I also know she can go overboard sometimes with reminding you about school, but you are doing a great job. You'll be fine, sis. We're all survivors trying to navigate through this world."

Suddenly, I understood. I was a survivor. Mom was a survivor. She survived raising me and my siblings. Dad worked hard to provide for all of us. Maybe I just hadn't had an opportunity to understand my parents better, but I hoped to get there eventually.

Linh and I sat for a while, and then she asked if I wanted to join her in painting. I agreed and we sat side by side at her desk. I picked up my brush, dipped it into the water and followed along with Linh's guidance.

"You know, you could be a teacher, Linh," I suggested eagerly. "You're guiding me so well," I said after I had begun my painting.

"Thanks Mai. I've never considered it, but maybe I should." Linh smiled widely, her cheeks blushing pink at the compliment. I was starting to feel less isolated, and I knew only time and patience would heal all the wounds I had with my mother.

We finished painting and I showed Linh my picture of flowers and leaves, painted in bright colors.

"Wow, you're pretty good for a beginner," she said in surprise.

"I think I got it from you." I chuckled.

"How do you feel?" Linh asked. I had always been close to Như and Hồng-an, so I was glad to have this opportunity to spend time with Linh.

"I'm much better. Thanks." I reached out to hug her once again, realizing I was slowly letting go of the old feelings of uneasiness and trauma.

CHAPTER 19

BUMPS AND PROGRESS

On a late Monday afternoon, after I got home from school, I finally decided to make a phone call that would change my life. As I was about to grab my phone to call for a therapy appointment, Hồng-an walked to my room to check on me. She opened the door slowly and peeked in.

"Mai? Come with me to my room so we can call your therapist together."

I turned around from my desk. "Perfect timing, sis. I was just about to grab my phone and call. I am glad you checked on me."

I got up and headed over to my sister's room, being mindful of each step I took to avoid tripping. As we got to Hồng-an's room, she shut the door behind her and I hopped onto her bed.

"Do you mind calling her for me?"

"Mai, you can do it yourself. This is the opportunity to show your responsibility," Hồng-an gently encouraged me. I knew I could do it but was unsure of how I could take the first step since this phone call was going out of my comfort zone.

It suddenly hit me that up until now, I had not known how to make a simple phone call to ask for essential services. I had been too focused on writing, stressing out, and worrying about grades to care. Besides, my parents did all that for me, which left me anxious to step into advocating for myself.

"You're right. I'm capable."

"That's the spirit, Mai."

"I love you, Hồng-an."

"I love you too."

My fingers were shaking as I slowly dialed out the number. I held up the phone to my ear and waited as it rang three times. On the fourth ring, a pleasant voice picked up on the other end, introducing themselves as Maura. I hesitated for a moment, took a deep breath, and then relaxed as I spoke to the receptionist. After telling her what I was calling about, she put me on hold.

I stayed on the line through the tune of "Turkish March" by Mozart. The music was fast enough to help keep my mood in check while also holding me long enough to collect my thoughts. Finally, the music on the phone stopped and a new pleasant voice picked up.

"Hi, this is Luann." She spoke with calming gentleness. I immediately felt comfortable talking to her and as we spoke, I felt myself easing into the conversation more and more. After sharing a few details about myself and answering some questions, I made my appointment with Luann, thanked her, and hung up the phone, feeling more confident now that I had taken the first step to getting help all by myself. I flopped back onto the bed and heaved a big sigh, relief washing over me.

Hồng-an had been watching me the entire time and she smiled proudly at me. "See, Mai, that wasn't so bad. You did it!"

"Thanks for the encouragement. I appreciate it."

I walked with Hồng-an downstairs after making the appointment, where we were greeted by our parents and the rest of the siblings. My mother was surprised to see me downstairs, as I was usually holed up in my room these days doing assignments.

"Oh, this is new. I am so used to you not coming downstairs until dinner time," my mom commented. I frowned slightly, looking at Hông-an for reassurance.

"Mai got help today. Well, I mean, she made an appointment to talk to someone," Hông-an spoke up for me.

"That's good, Mai. I'm glad you're taking care of yourself," my father said, stepping forward to give me a reassuring pat. My mother didn't say a word. Instead, she got up from the table where she had been sitting, walked to the kitchen, turned on the stove, got out a pan, and started cooking. While my mom cooked, the rest of my siblings and I hung out in the dining room in relative silence, everyone feeling the tension that seemed to be pouring off my mother even from the kitchen. My father let out a low, awkward chuckle and shuffled off into the living room. Slowly my siblings and I began to chat about nothing in particular, and a few minutes later my mom came out of the kitchen with a fried egg sandwich in hand.

"Here, eat up. Then go study for your SAT practice test, Mai. You got lots to do. No need to sit and waste time." I shot my siblings a look that said *I told you so.*

"Yes, mother." I glanced at the clock to distract myself and to keep from reacting.

"Time is very valuable. Make sure you don't waste a minute." She spoke sternly. I knew she wanted to say more, but she stopped herself just in time.

I rolled my eyes, unable to take the annoyance any longer.

I hurriedly finished my food and went upstairs to my room to avoid any further issues with my mother. I closed the door and turned to my desk, which was covered with my notes, books, and plans for senior year. I had only one more year to go until I could go off to college without her nagging me so often. I looked over at my class selection form, the blank lines seeming to jump off the page at me. I stared at it for a long while in silence before closing my eyes to pray.

Dear Lord, please grant me the strength to pick my classes wisely, help my family to be peaceful, and for me to know you better so that I can follow your will. Amen.

I opened my eyes and moved to sit down at my desk. I then took out my journal and began to write.

School.
Books, finals, homework, activities
fifteen years, it ruled my life.
One year
then I'm tossed into the hands of Reality.

Where do I go?
When all I do is decide,
all I do is write,
all I do is wait.
My future is looming,
There are many expectations.

I want to follow my passion.
Sometimes mistaken for simple infatuation.
It is more,
I will be more.
Dreams are meant to be followed.

School is a haven but also a pain.
Afraid of failing,
Or is it just a mindset?
My mom can rage on:
You can't fail, you have to try!

I am vulnerable.
I just want my destiny,
live what they call life.
Adventure, risk, experience
I have a thousand dreams
of roaming worlds.

Life is also a Teacher,
experience a Sister,
wisdom a mother.
Adventure is a guide,
risk a friend,
and happiness a lover.

I am the Bearer of all,
In the end,
only my soul can judge,
my mind understand,
and my heart say,
That I lived to my fullest.
-Some things they don't teach in books.

It was then that I realized the impact of my words on paper. My mother might say otherwise, but at this moment, I felt better. It was a poem that sprung from my mind and soul.

Come, it seemed to beckon. *Feel me to the depths of your heart.*

And for a moment I stopped. I listened. I felt.

***

On a Wednesday afternoon, Như picked me up after class. As soon as I stepped out of the school gate heading toward the parking lot, I heard a honk. Turning my head, I saw my sister sitting in her car near the curb, waving at me through the window.

"Hey, I'm over here! C'mon, I don't want you to be late for your first therapy appointment!" Như hollered at me.

"I'm coming!" I made my way to the car quickly, opened the door and hopped in.

"Here, let me help you with the seat belt," Minh reached over and pulled the belt toward me.

"Thanks, bro." I gave him a pat on the back.

"No biggie, we're here for you."

Như pulled onto the freeway and a few minutes later, she parked the car in front of a big, bright yellow building. Sprawled across the building were the words SUNSHINE WELLNESS CLINIC. My siblings and I walked into the air-conditioned office, and a lady dressed in a polka dot outfit greeted us cheerfully.

"Hello, I'm Maura. Please have a seat." Maura handed me some forms to fill out.

"Thank you so much." I filled out the forms, reading the list of symptoms and then checking off boxes that applied. A few minutes later, a lady dressed in a casual yellow outfit stepped out from the left side door and came over to greet me.

"*Chào con, cô tên là* Luann. Hello, my name is Luann." I was surprised for a moment, as I had forgotten the urgent care doctor had told me she could speak Vietnamese. She also did not look Vietnamese; her skin was pale, and she had light-brown eyes with reddish-brown hair. I briefly wondered if she was half Vietnamese but realized it really didn't matter.

"*Chào cô*—Hello." I placed my hand in hers and felt a firm grasp.

"Come right this way to my office, Mai." Luann extended her other hand out to help me stand.

"No, I can manage. Thanks." I followed her to the office.

"Please, have a seat." I sat in the comfy chair she had motioned to and once I was settled, she sat down too, focusing on me with her full attention. "So, tell me about what's going on."

"I'm going through a lot right now. It's kinda hard to talk about it."

"That's what I am here for," Luann said, reaching out toward her desk to hand me a stress ball. I took a deep breath and accepted the stress ball from her.

"Um. I've been stressing out about schoolwork, but mainly just trying to decide if I want to go into a medical career or pursue writing. It has been difficult because my mom is on the fence about the idea."

"That must be really rough," Luann replied with empathy.

"Yes, the hard part is convincing her that pursuing the arts, such as writing, and other humanities careers, matter just as much as STEM careers."

"I see what you are saying, Mai. How do you want to tell your mom how you feel?"

"Well at times, the conversations can be difficult because for one thing, my mom's idea of success is to be a medical professional. This notion is harmful to me, and I would guess it contributed to the indecisiveness and insecurity of my own calling in life," I said, finally letting out a long breath.

Luann's eyes perked up. "You just identified the root of your struggles. Good call, Mai, good call."

"Thanks." I felt myself calming down.

"Have you ever thought about reaching out to her and setting up boundaries?" Luann asked, pausing in between for me to respond.

"I guess I never thought of it that way."

"Mai, your mom lived in a different generation. Her generation had to deal with a lot of conflicts. Nowadays, I can see why young people like you get so worked up about pleasing your parents." Luann leaned over to turn on the fan near her desk. She continued, "When you get depression and anxiety, it is because you are dealing with a different set of conflicts. You are almost a senior in high school, nearing adulthood, and trying to find your way in the world."

"I think that is more like how I feel at the moment. Thank you for helping me clarify my feelings."

"Take a deep breath, Mai. Inhale and then exhale. Count to ten for each breath. You can also use your five senses to bring yourself back to the present moment. Have you ever tried meditation to help relax and focus your mind?"

"No. I haven't really thought of that."

"Well, meditation can help you focus your mind. It also has its roots in Buddhism. Pretty cool, huh?"

"Yeah, my mom was a Buddhist until she converted to Catholicism upon marriage to my dad."

"Oh, that's cool, Mai. Do you go to both a church and a temple every week?"

"No, since my mom converted, it was a lot easier to go to Mass."

"Do you ever feel stuck in between when you go?"

"What do you mean? Like have I ever been uncomfortable about my faith?"

"Yes, somewhere along those lines."

"I actually never really thought about that, except for one thing. When my mom says something, she never seemed to hear my side of the story. Like this anxiety attack incident perhaps. She couldn't believe it when I tried to talk to her about my schoolwork, career plans, and just the expectations of being the youngest child with cerebral palsy."

"I see. So she's overprotective of you because she worries you won't be able to do things by yourself?"

I nodded. "Yes, I just want to show her I am capable of pursuing other career paths too. Also, she seems to be against me taking medication for mental health because it's a cultural issue. She thinks therapy and medication are not going to help much. So, I think my physical disability and my mental health somehow has a connection to her fear of letting go."

"Bingo. That could be a possibility, Mai," Luann said, her eyes twinkling with compassion.

"So how can I mend my relationship with my mom?" I asked, feeling relieved now.

"Well, you can meditate and pray how you wish, and you can still take medication. Do you want me to talk to your mom about it?"

"I'd rather wait. I'll talk to her myself."

"Okay, let me know if you need my help. On the other hand, your mom might be going through some feelings of desolation," Luann said, making herself comfortable in her chair.

"Can you explain more about that for me?"

"Sure, Mai. Your mom is going through a realization that you're growing up and to her, you're still her little girl, even though you're almost an adult."

I took a deep breath again and slowly let it out. "I think I forgot my mom was once a teen too. It's hard to believe she came from a different generation and country. She probably went through a lot more hardships."

I had a moment of epiphany.

I saw my mother as a woman who, in her efforts to raise her six children, was struggling to show her vulnerability and bond with her children. I saw her as a flawed human being but still my mother, regardless of our relationship. Tears fell from my eyes as I thought about it more. Luann handed me a Kleenex without a word. For a moment, I sat in silence with Luann as I processed my feelings.

Luann added, "Your mom also cared about you the way she knew how. She didn't have the luxury to stress over things. It just means her struggles gave her the strength and a different way to cope with life."

"I understand now," I said, grateful for the clarification.

"Your mom will get there. Give her time to come to you."

"Thanks again."

As I got ready to leave, Luann scheduled another therapy appointment for two weeks later and we concluded our first session. My mood had lifted since I had first came in. I walked back out to the waiting room where my siblings were still waiting.

"All done with your session?" Như asked, leaning over to give me a hug. My other siblings stood up and followed us out of the clinic.

"Yup, I had a really good conversation with Luann. She's really nice and empathetic." I explained.

"I'm glad," Như replied as we got into the car and drove home.

CHAPTER 20

HEALING THE WOUNDS

My siblings and I drove home to our parents waiting for us at the door of our house. I took off my shoes carefully to avoid tripping. "Mom?" I asked, reluctantly waiting for her to respond. Deep down I felt timid, like a scared puppy afraid that at any moment my mother would lecture me again. If it wasn't about me working hard to get into a great college, it was some other matter to trigger my inner helplessness.

"Do you need something, honey?" she asked, careful to avoid lecturing me. I expected she would say something along the lines of "Why are you home late?" or "What took you so long?" in her usual panicky voice.

"Can we talk?" I looked up at her, unsure of what her reaction would be. I managed to give her a tiny smile, but I did not dare to say anything further. It was the anticipation that sent goosebumps down my back. Despite my mother's care through her acts of service, I found myself unable to communicate with her, which set off my defense mechanism.

"Yes, let's go to your room." My mother walked behind me as I made my way up the stairs. I held on to the stair rails to keep from losing my balance. As we got to my bedroom, I closed the door and sat down on my bed across from my mother, making eye contact with her.

"Mom, first of all, I just want to say I am sorry," I began, hesitating on the next words. It had been a long time coming. "I know you're probably feeling like I don't appreciate you enough and I know you want me to do well in life. I understand the very real fear of how you could take care of me because of my physical limitations. Well, I have my own capabilities and I am not limited in any way because I have what I need, and that's the support of our family."

My mother nodded and gestured for me to continue. She kept a straight face, but I could see she was struggling to react properly. She crossed her arms and made eye contact with me.

"I understand each family dynamic is different and no family is perfect. We can all learn something from each other and make our past pain better." I spoke calmly, moving closer to my mother and putting my hands in hers.

In that moment, she burst into tears. I could see her wrinkled face now. As I grasped her hand, I looked down to see the creases on them. A tiny pang of fear took me by surprise as I realized she was aging. My mother paused, calming her tears and taking a few deep breaths before replying.

"Honey, no. I am sorry. I am sorry for putting so much pressure on you all these years to succeed. I wanted you to succeed my way, but I wasn't letting you grow." Her lips curved into a sad smile. For the first time in my life, I saw her at her most vulnerable.

It was the little girl inside of her who struggled to get validation from other people in my family. That was why she didn't want me to endure the painful consequences of having a hard life. Like every parent, she expected me to succeed and sought to form ideas of what she wanted for her children. That was why she was so hard on herself and tough with me to the point of being overprotective.

"Mom, I realized something. You were just trying your best to care for me in the only way you knew how because you and Dad came from a different upbringing. Also, I think I understand why you feel the way you feel." I laid down on my bed now with her by my side, caressing my hair every once in a while. She really did love me, though maybe it was slightly flawed love because she was still healing from her own trauma. "I know it is a hard truth to hear, but I own my feelings. I know we need to heal. The past is past."

"Yes, Mai. I apologize for underestimating your capabilities. I feel bad that I forced you to be someone you're not." My mother lay down next to me, hugging me toward her like she did when I was a baby. I was no longer a baby physically, but I knew her embrace was her way of taking in the last of my little girl years.

"Mom, I know you and Dad raised us to be our own people, and I am glad you're finally realizing my needs. It's progress. Also, I know you were adjusting to raising me as the youngest daughter with cerebral palsy." I turned to her now, wrapping my arms around her tummy, and we stared up at the ceiling in silence. Immediately, I was transported back to my younger years of sleeping next to her before having my own room.

"Well, it's true. I have a long way to go. Your disability should not affect your capability to do things," my mother said, wiping away visible tears on her face.

"It's actually more than that. Like, I actually want to pursue writing because I believe I can make it in the world career-wise. I don't think a successful career has to be limited to just being a medical professional. I mean, I write and I write from my heart. Isn't that what being myself is all about? It's sticking to the true self that matters to me much more than the notion of having a career that is more prestigious than others. Như is prepping to be a doctor because that's her calling; my calling is writing."

"I understand now, Mai." She nodded, tightening her arms around me as we lay next to each other.

"Know that I'm still your daughter. I am still practicing my faith, and still doing my best in school. In fact, my therapist even suggested I should go for spiritual direction in addition to her appointments with me." I grinned now, surprised at the progress we had made in bonding.

"I see. She's helpful to you," my mother said, nodding her head.

"Also, about the time you threw my journal down when you saw me writing, that definitely hurt my heart. I know you didn't mean it, but I have to be honest with you. I wasn't expecting that kind of backlash. My worst nightmare came true." *I forgive you, Mom.* I thought it but didn't dare say it aloud. I needed to trust her. My mother sat up now. Tears again filled her eyes and I leaned forward with my arms wide open, embracing her and letting myself feel like a child she had once carried. "It's okay, Mom. I know you care. This is going to take time for us to adjust to."

"Right. Do you need a moment, Mai?"

"We can keep talking if you want," I said, hugging her once again.

"I want to give you some space. Oh wait. Do you want to show me one of your poems?"

"I thought you'd never ask. Let me go get my journal."

"Sure, Mai." My mother looked down and touched my pink bedspread. "You know, I've always wanted a bedroom like yours. Growing up poor in Vietnam led me to America and because of that, I wanted you to benefit from the opportunities."

"Mom, it's already a big sacrifice that you are here. You know that. But dreams do not have to be limited to just a certain career. We can do what we love, practice mental well-being, and develop relationships."

"Yes," my mother nodded, pausing to let me continue. She looked deep in thought.

"Also, we can still get professional help and not feel like we're unheard. I also know I wouldn't be here if it wasn't for God. I know God sees my struggles and that's why He blessed me with Luann to help me sort through the roots of my insecurities, so I can have a better relationship with you, Dad, and my siblings. Through this journey, I feel He is with me always." I could feel my confidence rising as I transitioned into this deeper bond with her. "You know, Mom, I thought I would take a long time to open up to you, but it looks like we are doing just fine. Thank you for letting me talk."

"Yes, Mai, I believe that's true. You're such a beacon of strength."

"Mom, you know who I got it from, and I think it's also mindful that we step away from viewing me as an inspiration. I am not your trophy child. I am trying to live my passion and find myself. But the love I have for my family is my light, and that brightness will never ever die out," I responded, feeling a huge weight lifted off my shoulders.

I took out my journal and flipped to the first poem, "Here Mom, take a look." My voice rose with excitement as I finally showed her my poems.

My mother's eyes scanned the page as I watched for her reaction. Her mouth hung open and her face shifted from surprised to a state of shock. Her lips quivered with emotion and her eyebrows curved as she read silently to herself. She muttered softly and placed her hand over her chest. I saw her shoulders shaking slightly up and down.

A Sonnet to My Mother
Comforter by nature; her womb housed me,
Sleepless nights and hard workdays.
Caregiver to my health; wiper of tears.
Resilient child protected from dying,
Instinct's eye is visible now,
Sweet bird songs fill the air,
Her voice bearing an angel's perfect hymn
Devotion since she got my father's ring.

My mom's eyes were watering by the time she finished reading these lines. I handed her the tissue box near my desk. She plucked a tissue out of the box and batted them at her eyes.

"Mai, this is so beautiful. I am so impressed. How did you come up with these words?" my mother asked, her face bursting with amazement. I didn't say a word but continued showing her more of my poetry.

"Wow, you really are talented. I'm so proud of you," my mother said, beaming now. She had read through a few more of my poems and seemed genuinely interested in them.

"Thanks, Mom. I never thought I'd hear you say I'm talented. Does that mean I can go into writing in the future?" I asked her hopefully.

"Well, you do you," she replied with a smile. I returned it and we went back to reading the poems and stories that filled the pages of my journal.

***

I shut my bedroom door for some alone time once my mother had left my room. There had been such a big change from the mother I knew before, and I felt relieved to know we could finally talk to one another. I could only hope things continued in this way into the future and decided to pray for my mother.

"Dear Lord, help me learn to forgive and love my mother as she is. Help her know how to be patient as I am maturing physically and spiritually. Give her the heart to love and hold dear my dreams. Amen."

I walked over to my desk as a feeling of relief washed over me. I took my time to arrange my books neatly in rows as I cleared my desk of the clutter. Satisfied with my mess-free desk, I walked downstairs to retrieve a washcloth, and then went up the stairs again. With a trash bag in hand, I cleaned every corner of my room and made my bed as neatly as I could.

The first step to healing internally was clearing out the clutter to make room for space to sit and be still, take in all my surroundings and practice gratitude. *I'll make it to college. I know I can.* After all, nothing was impossible when there was support for me.

CHAPTER 21

A HOPEFUL FUTURE

Junior year passed uneventfully, and it was soon my last year of high school. I spent time reflecting on myself and my relationship with my family, but most importantly with my mother. Since that first appointment with Luann, I learned the art of setting boundaries. I also wrote tons of journal entries, reflected, and prayed more frequently thanks to Father Josef's strong spiritual guidance. I felt things were looking up for me.

On a bright Wednesday afternoon, Như and the rest of my sisters drove me to church again. As soon as Như parked the car, we all walked in together where Father Josef greeted us with all with a smile.

"Hi, girls! How are you doing? I've been praying for you all. Mai, are you here to see me?" he asked excitedly. I saw there was already a bible in his hand.

"Yes, indeed, Father. How did you know? I asked, grinning from ear to ear.

"I had a hunch you would come and see me today," Father Josef said, chuckling a bit. "Come this way to my office."

Father Josef led me to his office and left the door slightly ajar. He and I talked a while and I updated him that I had gone to therapy before seeing him.

"I am so pleased to hear you are getting the help you need. You can find God everywhere if you look closely." Father Josef leaned over to grab a book on Ignatian spirituality on his desk.

"Like where can I find God? It's so difficult to see and hear God sometimes," I admitted, feeling tears starting to fall. "I'm sorry, I don't mean to cry. It's just—" I paused to collect myself.

"No, no, no. Your tears are valid and you are in the healing process. It takes courage to be vulnerable and connect with your inner self, you know. That's a difficult thing to do, but you have courage. That courage is the seed for your faith to grow, Mai."

"Wow. That's a beautiful way to put it, Father. Thank you." I felt the love and the warmth from the priest easing my way back into my faith.

Father Josef pointed to the window near his desk. "See the bright sun shining and the white clouds?"

I stood up and got closer to the window. "Yes, Father. It's so pretty."

"That beauty is from God, Mai. He knows what you need. So when you feel down, depressed, or when life feels too much to handle, you can look up the sky and find God there. You can find Him in your interactions with family and friends. They are there for you. There's a motto in Latin called *ad majoriam deo gloriam*. It means for the glory of God. That's what 'finding God in all things' is. He meets you at your most painful moments and He also loves you unconditionally and eternally," Father Josef explained, his eyes twinkling and dancing with glee.

I smiled. "God sure does love me, right Father? Even when I trip up sometimes?" I relaxed now, feeling my confidence rising.

"Absolutely, Mai! He will bless you as you figure out His gifts for you. I'm proud of you. God is always patient and kind. He waits for you to come to him." Father Josef clasped his hands together. "Dear Loving Father, please bless Mai and give her the strength to come to you."

"Also, can you pray for a passing score on my SAT test, please?" I asked.

"Absolutely!" Father Josef's voice rang like bells on Christmas as he reached over to his desk for his prayer journal and pen, scribbling my prayer request down.

"Thank you so much for being here for me, Father." I closed my eyes at this point, reflecting on the silence with him.

Father Josef remained silent and deep in prayer with his eyes closed for a few more minutes until he finally opened his eyes. He placed his hand over me and gave me a blessing before sending me on my way.

I could feel the positive energy rising and warming my soul as I walked out to my siblings waiting for me in the pews.

"I'm done." I broke into a wide smile and then stood up, turning toward the altar and making a sign of the cross before making my way out of the church, followed by my siblings.

***

On a bright Thursday afternoon after school, my siblings drove me to the therapy appointment where I ran in and was greeted by Luann again.

"How are you doing today?" Luann asked, handing me a cookie. I liked that she always kept treats to make her patients feel at home. She wore a blue, striped shirt and jeans with flowers on the corners of her pockets

"I am doing so much better than I thought." I beamed eagerly, folding my hands together in my lap. "I think I came a long way since the first therapy session started."

"That's good. I am glad to hear that." Luann perked up, grinning widely now. "Have you decided where you're going to apply for college yet?" She asked again, all ears to hear my plan for college.

"Good question. I actually haven't thought about it that much. But I plan on majoring in English. Speaking of that, guess what?" I asked her, trying to hold in my excitement. My stomach fluttered and there was a brief roller-coaster, flip-flop sensation inside me.

"What is it?" Luann's eyes twinkled with eagerness

"I did the challenge you gave me and I'm taking my SAT exam next week!" I shouted now, getting up to dance around her office.

"Oh, really? Did you talk to your mom? And good luck on your exam! I'm sending you all the positive vibes. You got this!" Luann's face lit up like she had just won a lottery with me.

"Yes!" I said, louder and with passion now. I giggled like a little girl showing off her skills in the playground.

"Congratulations, Mai. What did you tell your mom?"

I filled Luann in on my conversation with my mother. The time went by quickly as I became engrossed in opening up to her. She nodded occasionally, taking brief pauses in between as I talked. "I think she finally understood what I was talking about. And she also apologized to me."

"Wow, that's better progress than I initially set out for you to do. I'm so proud of how far you have come in your mental health journey. It's definitely something you should keep up." Luann said, smiling with her eyes.

"I will. Thank you so much for helping me. I couldn't have done it without you." Those old, repressed feelings were slowly healing as I felt my self-esteem rising.

"Aww, Mai, you did it all on your own. I'm just there for the journey. Keep taking care of yourself," Luann said, locking thumbs with me.

"Oh, Luann, guess what? I got spiritual direction too. I've been seeing a priest in my local parish. I have this one priest who I really like. He's so into writing and I think he just has a great outlook on spirituality and life in general. He's a Jesuit priest," I said, my voice rising with excitement now.

"That's great. I'm so glad. May I ask you what his name is?"

"Sure, his name is Father Josef. He has a deep sense of spirituality and he's just so passionate about God. He showed me similar ways to yours on how to rekindle my relationship with my mom. He's also into Ignatian spirituality. I like to think that you helped me with the psychological side of my feelings while he helped me on the spiritual side and that's a win-win."

"I'm glad you finally found someone to help you with this aspect of your life. Take lots of time for self-care and you're well on your way. Follow your passion. Don't be afraid to step out of your comfort zone." Luann leaned over to her desk and took a small rock. She handed it to me. "Here, feel this rock in your hand. Is it hard when you touch it?"

"Yeah, it's hard to the touch," I answered her eagerly.

Luann extended her hand out and I handed her back the rock. "That's how your heart feels when you're not being heard. It's difficult for you to open up because you needed to trust someone."

"Wow, that's a really good metaphor. Thanks. May I show you a poem I wrote?" I asked, reaching behind my chair to grab my blue poetry journal from my purse. "Here's the first one." I grinned excitedly.

"Okay, Go ahead and share, Mai." Luann said, eagerly waiting.

I handed her my journal. She flipped through the journal and came across several poems.

"I have the one about one of my favorite television grandfathers. It's called Mister Rogers."

> *Mister Rogers*
> *As you inspire generations of children to be kind,*
> *Singing the song of "Could you be mine?"*
> *Encouraging our confidence to shine,*
> *In a world where it's hard to be yourself,*
> *You taught us about love from above.*
> *When all things seem to be going wrong,*
> *How to express our feelings in a healthy way,*
> *As we live each day,*
> *How joyful to come home every afternoon,*
> *Turn on the channel,*
> *To see your smiling face!*

"Wow, that's really amazing. You definitely have a gift, Mai. Great job." I smiled at her, grateful for her acknowledgment. "Thank you so much for sharing," Luann said, crying now. She reached over to her desk and grabbed a Kleenex, batting at her eyes.

"Oh, gosh, I didn't mean to make you cry. I always thought therapists didn't cry." I stammered a bit now, my face blushing red with embarrassment.

"No, no, these poems are so beautiful. You really touched my heart and soul, Mai. I've never seen such talent coming from young people like you. Your writing and voice are so unique in that they give me a deep sense of gratitude." Luann took her hand in mine and we looked at each other in appreciation.

"Thank you, I'm so flattered. You're the best therapist ever."

"Wow, you are so talented. Your words seem to flow out of the page when you write these poems. It's definitely your God-given talent. Thank you for sharing these poems with me, Mai."

"You're welcome, Luann."

"Let me walk you out. Do you need help with your bag?" Luann asked, extending her hand out.

"I am good, but you can walk me out," I said, accepting her kind offer.

Luann and I walked out to my sister Như and the rest of my siblings waiting for me in the lobby. A feeling of relief washed over me as I realized for the first time in my life that I felt truly understood. *That's why my parents gave me the nickname "Perseverance."* I smiled as I thought.

***

A week after my therapist appointment, Hồng-an dropped me off at school for my SAT exam and I walked in, carrying my backpack with all the testing materials. As soon as the testing proctor gave us the go-ahead, I said a quick Hail Mary and then proceeded to focus entirely on my test. Two hours later, I completed the test, mouthed the test proctor a quick goodbye, and then headed out to the car where Hồng-an waited for me.

"How was the exam?" Hồng-an asked as I opened the car door and buckled up. She put her keys in the ignition and then we were on our way.

"The test went well. I hope I got a good score, but I am fine with any score. No need for me to stress over too many things. Besides, whatever score I have, I will take it. Test scores don't even tell the whole picture of who I am. I just know I'll make it to college no matter what I get," I said confidently.

Hồng-an smiled. "Wow, what an incredible shift in perspective. I'm so proud of you, Mai. Therapy is working wonders and you have come a long way."

I smiled wider now, grateful for my sister's acknowledgment. "Thanks," I stammered, my face blushing red.

"You did it yourself. You've climbed up that mountain. Now you just need to wait for the results," Hồng-an said as she headed toward our street. She stopped and parked the car in the driveway and then turned to me, making eye contact. "The future is yours, Mai. Follow your dreams."

"I will." I nodded more surely this time.

I got my test results in the mail later that week and came out with an above average score.

It truly takes a village.

CHAPTER 22
AT FULL BRIGHTNESS

My mother picked me up from school in the afternoon and drove me to church.

"Let me know when you are done with your spiritual direction session. I'll wait in the car."

"Okay, Mom," I said, opening the door and getting out slowly to avoid tripping.

"Be safe. God is with you. I'm so proud of you for progressing in life. You're going to make strides in college. You are going to write great things. Just bare your soul and God will take care of the rest." She looked at me with pride and I felt my heart swell with happiness. We had worked so hard to rekindle our relationship.

"Thanks, Mom." I leaned back into the car to give her a quick kiss, closed the car door and headed into the church.

I knew I had come a long way since my junior year. A lot had happened in a year, and I felt proud of my accomplishments. It hadn't been an entirely easy path to walk though, and in my most difficult moments, I always thought of how far I had already come and how my faith was shaping me. My therapist had helped me learn to cope with my stress and feelings of insecurities, while Father Josef always made sure I knew I was not alone and God was always on my side.

On that day as I stepped into the church, a warm feeling washed over me.

"Hi Father Josef! I'm so glad to see you!" My voice boomed over the empty church.

"Mai! How are you?" he asked, grinning from ear to ear. He was in the front pew, waiting for me in his clerics as usual. The church was usually packed with people on other days, but today was quiet and peaceful. The brown doors were wide open, and the afternoon sun shone on the stained-glass image of the Holy Spirit dove as I walked in.

"I am doing well," I said, moving to sit beside him in the pew and eager to update him on my life. I smiled widely, knowing my faith was restored. Father Josef had this way about him that he made everyone feel comfortable to open up about their life stories to him.

"So tell me, what has been going on in your life? What has God been telling you these past weeks?" he asked, reaching over to pick up the bible he had sitting beside him.

"Well, I met with my therapist a couple times and she helped me work through my feelings. She also mentioned I should get spiritual direction, which I am so glad to do, because I found you. Oh, and my mom and I are on better terms. Thanks for always praying for me and my family. I also had a high score in my SAT tests! It has been a long journey to get to this healing process. I cannot believe it's my senior year and I am going to college next year."

"I love that! And I can already see God is working in your life."

"God is something else. He does things when I least expect it. I'm so impatient sometimes." I nodded, laying my hands on my lap.

"God is working even if you are impatient. He loves and forgives you, Mai."

"Thanks, Father. Do you think God knows his plans for me?"

Father Josef opened the bible. "What is your heart telling you Mai? What is God speaking to you at this moment in time? How do you feel when you write?"

"Wow, I never really thought about it that deeply. Thank you for bringing that up, Father."

"You're very welcome. I know you've heard of Ignatian spirituality during our previous session," Father Josef said, smiling wider now.

"Yes, Father, it's finding God in all things," I replied, feeling a sense of calmness wash through me. Father Josef smiled and handed me a small prayer card. On the card was a picture of St. Ignatius with the words *ad majorem deo gloriam* and beneath that it said,

> The Examen:
> Ask God for graces
> Give thanks
> Review the day
> Face your shortcomings
> Look forward to the next day.

"Wow, thanks Father. It's like when my therapist Luann showed me how to bring myself to the present moment. So no long prayers like the rosary?" I asked, finally realizing there are different methods to talk to God.

"Well, you can still pray the rosary, but this is another form of prayer you can do. It's shorter and it only takes a few minutes out of your day. You can even use your journal to do it. I want you to remember that in this way, you are loved by God no matter what. You should also remember that when you write from your heart, you are allowing yourself to be led by love. That's what Jesus wants for you," Father Josef said, putting the bible back down.

"Thank you for reminding me to find God in all things, Father."

"You're welcome, Mai.

"You know, I struggled with whether or not I should go into writing or follow a different path for my career for a long time," I admitted.

"God saw your pain and He knows what you need now. Follow your heart, and it will never lead you wrong," Father Josef replied. "Stay true to yourself. I'll keep you in my prayers. Remember that you are a bright light in those who know you. Keep shining and being you."

"I will!" I said enthusiastically, jumping to my feet in my happiness. Father Josef laughed as he stood up as well. "Thank you again, Father," I said, making my way toward the church doors.

"I am always happy to help. May God bless you, Mai." He walked me to the doors of the church, and I waved to him as I headed out into the parking lot and toward my mother's waiting car.

"All done? How was your session with Father Josef?" my mother asked as I climbed into the car, eager to hear about my time with him.

"The session went well. He gave me a lot of tips for spiritual self-care." I leaned over a bit to give her a side hug, which she returned happily. For the first time in my life, I could feel the overwhelming pure love from my heart.

"I'm proud of you, Mai." She pulled back and I could see her eyes shimmering with tears. "Thank you for teaching me that life matters much more when we dive into doing something we love." Her tears fell down her cheeks, but I knew this time they were tears of joy. I cried in happiness with her.

Once we had composed ourselves, my mother drove us to a little public garden near our house. The garden was a beautiful and peaceful place, filled with roses, tulips, and daisies. We both got out of the car and looked out over the garden, watching as the sunset on the horizon casted a beautiful mix of purple, orange, and pink.

"Look, Mai. Isn't the sky beautiful?" My mother marveled at the brightness of the slowly fading day.

"Yes, I think God is trying to tell us something, Mom. I pointed toward the sky as I wrapped my arms around her shoulder.

"What's that?" she wondered, looking up at where I pointed.

"We are loved unconditionally with all the scars, flaws, and gifts wrapped in this embrace of the soul. It moves us gently through life and caresses us through the tears and joy. That's what makes us strong. The strength comes from connecting with those we love, and forgiveness can turn into this beautiful gift of human vulnerability. And that's how we can understand each other through these storms of life," I whispered to her, hugging her even closer.

"You are wise beyond your years, sweetheart. Go pursue your dreams and write stories of your resilience; you are meant for this calling." She smiled encouragingly at me, but her eyes still carried a lingering sadness, as if she still felt bad for taking so long to reach this point with me.

"I forgive you, Mom. Please don't be too hard on yourself," I replied softly, taking her hand and grasping it tightly in my own, reassuring her of my love. I realized that with flaws and all, she was still the woman who raised me the best she could.

My mother and I looked at the beautiful sunset, arms locked as we breathed in the fresh air of the evening and enjoyed each other's presence in calming stillness. The sun's rays sparkled on the horizon at full brightness as I realized that we both healed from the darkness and found comfort in the light.

ACKNOWLEDGMENTS

In 2018, I did a TEDx Talk on perseverance. My big idea for this speech in front of a packed audience of five hundred people was simply this: *connection is the foundation for perseverance.* This book is the result of connections made throughout this publishing journey. When the whole world shut down due to the COVID-19 pandemic, I was finishing up a year of service in Americorps. While doing that, I scoured LinkedIn for jobs, hoping something would turn up. I scrolled up and down until I came across the Book Creators program.

Two years prior, I had self-published two books, both nonfiction and creative, so I decided to step out of those two mediums and try writing a fiction story. That's when I filled out the interest form and made the phone call, not really knowing what it would lead to. Lo and behold, this decision I made in June of 2020 turned out to be a wonderful decision!

To my family, thank you for all the sacrifices you all made to provide my siblings and I the resources to navigate life. Through the ups and downs, you have all been there for me through thick and thin.

To my siblings Tiffany, Annie, Telly, and Anthony, thank you for being sources of joy and accountability when I needed a big push to make this book a reality. In big ways and small, you provided company and priceless feedback while I worked hard at writing.

To my great-aunt, Bà Thược, thank you for providing food to keep me full while I was working on this project. Most of all, thank you for taking care of my family. Your love reminds me of my roots and as a Vietnamese who prides herself in knowing two languages. When I speak Vietnamese with you, I am reminded of the beauty of language, conversations, and the people back in Vietnam.

Thank you to my educators, most notably Ms. Evelyn Gonzales, who never gave up on me and wasn't afraid to be blunt when I needed to hear crucial life advice. Mrs. Cherie Harms, who supported me throughout my school journey, attending almost every graduation and taking me to countless lunches where you held space for my many heart-to-heart conversations. Mrs. McNelis, who believed in me when I doubted myself; you are one of the reasons I am inspired to continue to write like I do now. Mr. Todd Seal, I hope you remembered me as a senior in your English class! On the last day of class, you wrote in my yearbook that you hoped to see "the works of Sue Do available in bookstores everywhere!" Well, here it is in physical form, a reality. I am blessed to have a great network of teachers whom I still keep in touch with. Thank you.

Thank you to my beta readers and conversationalists. Emma Ferrell, for the occasional phone calls, various suggestions in chapters, and support for my book. Anobella Eshoo, for believing in me and allowing me to read long chapters over the phone. Natalie Benrubi Ramsey, for checking in weekly and providing feedback as needed. Grace Lin-Cereghino, for believing in me and reviewing those chapters as best as you could. Kim Woo and Dr. Marc Santamaria, J.D., who allowed me to share my story and inspiration for the book with them. Joanne Nguyễn, for being a great friend and supporter; I am glad our love of writing and artistry has kept our friendship intact. And finally, to Zimmie Phạm, for reviewing my work and believing wholeheartedly in this book.

Thank you as well to Romellee Acio for the many conversations and for encouraging me through this long process of publishing. Your heart and care for others inspires me to be a better friend. To Vicky Gianella, who has been there for me since the early days of my teenage years. Our friendship defies the test of time. Thank you for being my forever friend and big sister from another mother. Thank you also to Thảo Lê and Aileen Quach for the many conversations, boba, and food trips to keep me sane.

Thank you to David Nguyễn for helping me with my personal marketing video for this book, reaching more connections, and telling me about the Asian Hustle Network. Thank you again for your friendship and expertise during this writing journey.

I would also like to acknowledge my spiritual mentors, Joe Kraemer, S.J., and the Jesuit Quad team for their many prayers and support! The fruits of your prayers made this book possible, even when I doubted myself at times. Thank you all for the wisdom shared.

To my Santa Clara University community, thank you for taking me in and preparing me well to take on this huge passion project. I am deeply grateful for all the experiences and memories during my two years there, and most especially to Dr. Juan Velasco for inspiring me to write better.

Another big thanks to the team at New Degree Press, especially Eric Koester for your support and believing in this book's potential. Because of you, I became an author for the third time. To Melody Delgado Lorbeer, my developmental editor who spent many weeks with me in the beginning stages bouncing off ideas and suggestions, Brian Bies for guiding me through the nuts and bolts of publishing, and Michelle Pollack, my marketing and revisions editor, for being patient with me through this whole revision process in spite of my many questions.

To my author cohort, thank you for being my cheerleaders, especially my fellow authors Grace Rector and Brenna Blaylock. I like to think that fate brought us together! In the weeks and months of this journey, we endured so much together. Thank you for being such awesome friends!

To all my backers who made this book possible; I could not have done it without your wonderful support. Thank you!

Kathy Hernandez	Julie Dang
Trúc-Quân Nguyễn	Grace Rector
Anna Trịnh	Claudelle Lê
Minh Nguyễn	Matisse Lê
Vân Đỗ	Claire Chow
Annie Đỗ	Sania Tong Argao
Kyla Cuaresma	Audrey Sunu
Tiffany Đỗ	Zimmie Phạm
Phong Đỗ	Evelyn Gonzales
Telly Đỗ	Laura Chandler
Romellee Acio	Evienne Luu
Sherry Hudson	Elieen Cruz
Emma Carpenter	Eric Koester
Claudia Blodgett	Shirley Liu
Anobella Eshoo	Ange Liu
Dana Kangas	Vicky Gianella
Emma Ferrell	Hạnh Nguyễn
Justine Ramos	Mariah Manzano

Caitlin Lyons
Brian McFadyen
Anjali Badwal
Grace Lin-Cereghino
Sammi Bennett
E. Ozie
Ann Nuno
Sara Schaefer
Natalie Nguyễn
Christina Spangberg
Michael Santos
Brigitte Cheng
Taleah Tyrell
Julia Green
Nancy Rocamora
Nancy Nguyễn
KD Lê
Thi Nguyễn
Terri McCluskey
Janette Perla
Lauren Alongi
David Nguyễn
Vivian Trương
Casey Xuereb
Tâm-Huyền Nguyễn
Joanne Nguyễn
Sharon Nguyễn
Duyên Nguyễn
Jeanette Uddenfeldt
Thảo Trần
Tamsen Kelly
Gina Hằng Nguyễn

Grace Song
Jimmy Trần
Thùy Nguyễn
Anne Nguyễn
Mỹ-Hạnh Nguyễn
Carlisha Washington
Trâm-Anh Trần
Summer Tobin
Tony Lâm
Ngân Trần
Eric Chan
Derek Nguyễn
Brenna Blaylock
Mailynh Phan
Kelly Coons
Cecilia Wessinger
Chris Cheung
Linh Nguyễn
Alisha Sehgal
Karen Chow
Cherie Harms
Sarah Bonini
Colleen Boyle
Yoo Jin Nam
An Bùi
Esther Young
Jennifer Van
Erika Rasmussen
Natalie Ramsey
Eoin Lyons
Châu Hùynh
Diệp Trần

Kyler Juarez
Lena Nguyễn
Iaisha Sadat
Dan Dương
Marthena Phan
Michelle Phạm
Alexa Smith

Jessica Nguyễn
Tim Trần
Zachary Trần
Khadijah Wynter
Lyndsey Kincaid
The Seaton Family
Hồng Hà Hoàng

Finally, I would like to give thanks to the Almighty God for always being there for me and bestowing upon me this gift of writing. I am truly blessed.

www.ingramcontent.com/pod-product-compliance
Lightning Source LLC
LaVergne TN
LVHW011822060526
838200LV00053B/3871